NMLS SAFE Mortgage Loan Originator Exam Content Outline Study Guide and Two Full-Length Practice Exams

Study More Efficiently

Bova Books LLC
BovaBooks@gmail.com

Thank you for your Purchase!

We are available for full support of your studies for any questions or comments you may have. Email us at:

BovaBooks@gmail.com

Be sure to go to Page 234 for instructions on how to access your downloadable pdf study guide

Copyright © 2022 by Bova Books LLC. All rights reserved. No part of this publication may be reproduced, stored, or transmitted, in any form or by any means electronic, mechanical, photocopying, recording or otherwise, without the prior written permission of the author.

The contents of this book are for educational purposes only. No liability will be assumed by the author and the information in this book shall not be used in a court of law.

Bova Books LLC is in no way affiliated with NMLS

Table of Contents   Page

I.	Exam Format	4
II.	Content Outline	5
III.	Study Guide	13
IV.	Practice Exam 1	118
V.	Practice Exam 2	150
VI.	Solutions	182
VII.	Answer Key	235

Exam Format and Expectations

Hello and thank you for your purchase. We are here for all of your studying needs on your way to passing the SAFE MLO exam. Please be sure to email us at BovaBooks@gmail.com for any questions you may have.

When developing our study material, our primary goal is to focus on the core concepts you need to know on test day. We develop our material exactly in line with the topics in the NMLS Content Outline, so you no longer have to waste time sieving through unnecessary material. Here is a breakdown of what to expect from the exam:

- The examination is multiple-choice, and you get 190 minutes for the exam.
- Be sure to answer every question since there is no penalty for guessing.
- There are 120 questions on the exam
- 5 of the questions are not scored; however, you will not know which these are so treat all of them as if they are real
- Passing Score is 75%

The exam is divided into five separate knowledge areas to determine which topics are necessary. The breakdown of the questions is as follows:

1. Federal Mortgage-related Laws (24%)

2. Uniform State Content (11%)

3. General Mortgage Knowledge (20%)

4. Mortgage Loan Origination Activities (27%)

5. Ethics (18%)

Content Outline	Page #
I. Federal Mortgage-related Laws (24%)	13

A. Real Estate Settlement Procedures Act (RESPA), 12 CFR Part 1024 (Regulation X)

1. RESPA origins and purpose; definition of "mortgage broker"
2. Applicable loan types
3. RESPA prohibitions, limitations, & exemptions
4. Settlement services
5. Required borrower information on application (Regulation X)
6. Foreclosure process
7. Initial escrow statements

B. Equal Credit Opportunity Act (ECOA), 12 CFR Part 1002 (Regulation B)

1. ECOA permissible acts
2. Factors that cannot be used to discriminate
3. Circumstances where a loan can be denied
4. Regulation B
5. Notifying borrower of action taken (timing)
6. Required disclosures when application denied
7. Adverse action: definition/examples/notifications/timing
8. Information required on the application; definition of "elderly"
9. Mortgage loan originator (MLO) actions when borrower refuses to provide race/gender information
10. Co-signer requirements
11. Acceptable income for loan review
12. Creditworthiness factors

C. Truth in Lending Act (TILA), 12 CFR Part 1026 (Regulation Z)

1. Purpose of TILA
2. Loans covered under TILA
3. Definitions including APR, finance charge, dwelling, residential mortgage loan
4. "Notice of right to rescind"; refinance rescind scenarios; defining "seller contributions"
5. Home Ownership and Equity Protection Act (HOEPA), high-cost mortgages (12 CFR 1026.32)
6. Higher-priced mortgage loans (12 CFR 1026.35)
7. MLO compensation (12 CFR 1026.36(d))

D. TILA-RESPA Integrated Disclosure Rule (TRID) ("Know Before You Owe")

1. Purpose of TRID
2. Loans covered under TRID
3. Loan estimates: facts, required information, charges/fees
4. Definition of "loan consummation"
5. Special information booklet
6. Closing Disclosure
7. Disclosures timing
8. MLO actions if TRID disclosure is incomplete
9. "Change of circumstances"
10. Information that must be provided to consumer upon request
11. Borrower's right to rescission
12. Annual escrow statement

E. Other Federal Laws and Guidelines

1. Home Mortgage Disclosure Act (HMDA), 12 CFR Part 1003 (Regulation C)
2. Fair Credit Reporting Act (FCRA)/Fair and Accurate Credit Transactions Act (FACTA) 15 USC §
1681 et seq.
3. Federal Trade Commission Red Flag rules, 16 CFR Part 681
4. Bank Secrecy Act/Anti-money Laundering (BSA/AML)
5. Gramm-Leach-Bliley Act (GLBA) – Privacy, Federal Trade Commission Safeguard Rules and DoNot-Call
6. Mortgage Acts and Practices – Advertising, 12 CFR Part 1014 (Regulation N)
7. Electronic Signatures in Global and National Commerce Act (E-Sign Act)
8. USA PATRIOT Act
9. Homeowners' Protection Act (Private Mortgage Insurance (PMI) Cancellation Act)
10. Dodd-Frank Act

F. Regulatory Authority

1. Consumer Financial Protection Bureau (CFPB)
2. Department of Housing and Urban Development (HUD)

II. Uniform State Content (11%)

A. SAFE Act and CSBS/AARMR Model State Law

    1. SAFE Act:

        a) General purpose and scope
        b) Documents to be filed for public record

    2. State Mortgage Regulatory Agencies:

        a) Regulatory powers and responsibilities
        b) NMLS Registry and relationship with state regulators
        c) Frequency of exams
        d) MLO unique identifiers
        e) CFPB authority and CFPB Loan Originator rule (dual compensation)

    3. License Law and Regulation:

        a) People required to be licensed
        b) MLO-licensed services
        c) Allowable activities by underwriters, clerical staff, and loan processors
        d) Entities requiring licensed MLO
        e) Businesses not required to be licensed (depository institutions)
        f) Licensee qualifications & application process:
            i. Pre-license education
            ii. Background checks
            iii. Other requirements
            iv. Felony charges
        g) Waiting period for test retakes
        h) Sponsorship requirement
        i) Definition of "MLO"
        j) Grounds for denying a license
        k) License maintenance:
            i. Renewal period
            ii. Continuing Education requirements
            iii. Maintaining an active license
            iv. Retaking 80-3 test if inactive
        l) NMLS requirements:
            i. Change of employment notifications
            ii. Required submissions/disclosures

iii. NMLS identifier requirements
m) Temporary Authority to Originate – Economic Growth, Regulatory Relief, and Consumer Protection Act

4. Compliance:

a) State regulator's authority to examine a licensee's books and records and interview employees
b) Prohibited acts:
i. Paying for real estate agent ads

III. GENERAL MORTGAGE KNOWLEDGE (20%) <u>58</u>

A. Qualified and Non-qualified Mortgage Programs

1. Qualified mortgages
2. Conventional/conforming
   a) Includes Fannie Mae and Freddie Mac
3. Government
   a) Includes FHA, VA, USDA
4. Conventional/nonconforming
   a) Jumbo, Alt-A
   b) Subprime mortgage
   c) Guidance on nontraditional mortgage product risk
   d) Non-qualified mortgage

B. Mortgage Loan Products

1. Fixed-rate mortgages
2. Adjustable-rate mortgages (ARMs)
3. Purchase money second mortgages
4. Balloon mortgages
5. Reverse mortgages
6. Home equity line of credit (HELOC)
7. Construction mortgages
8. Interest-only mortgages

C. Terms Used in the Mortgage Industry

1. Loan terms: subordinate loans, escrow accounts, lien, tolerances, rate lock agreement, table

funding
2. Disclosure terms: yield spread premiums, federal mortgage loans, servicing transfers, lender credits
3. Financial terms: discount points, 2-1 buy-down, loan-to-value (LTV) ratio, accrued interest, finance
charges, daily simple interest
4. General terms: subordination, conveyance, primary/secondary market, third-party providers,
assumable loan, APR

IV. MORTGAGE LOAN ORIGINATION ACTIVITIES (27%)   82

A. Loan Inquiry and Application Process Requirements

1. Loan inquiry process – includes required disclosures
2. Borrower application:
    a) Accepting applications
    b) Offering/negotiating terms
    c) Managing information
    d) Permissible questions
    e) Gift donors
3. Verification:
    a) Authorization forms
    b) Percentage of bank account assets attributable toward a loan application
    c) Verifying employment
4. Suitability of products & programs – reflecting the type of loan on a mortgage application
5. Accuracy (tolerances):
    a) Violation scenarios
    b) Zero tolerance service charges
    c) 10% tolerance service charges
6. Disclosure timing:
    a) "Know Before You Owe"
    b) Notification of action taken
    c) Early disclosures
    d) Affiliated business arrangements
7. Loan estimate timing:
    a) Initial Loan Estimate
    b) Revised Loan Estimate
    c) Expiration of Loan Estimate settlement charges

        d) Tolerance corrections
- 8. Closing Disclosure
  - a) Homeownership Counseling Disclosure

B. Qualification: Processing & Underwriting

1. Borrower Analysis:
   - a) Assets
   - b) Liabilities
   - c) Income
   - d) Credit report
   - e) Qualifying ratios (LTV, debt-to-income)
   - f) Ability to repay
2. Appraisals:
   - a) Purpose/definitions
   - b) Approaches (market, income, cost)
   - c) Timing
   - d) Independent appraisal requirement
3. Title Report:
   - a) Obtaining title reports
   - b) Timing of title reports and commitments
   - c) Preliminary title reports
4. Insurance:
   - a) Flood insurance
   - b) PMI
   - c) Hazard/homeowner insurance
   - d) Government mortgage insurance

C. Closing

1. Title and title insurance
2. Settlement/Closing Agent:
   - a) Eligible signatures on security instrument
   - b) Power of attorney
3. Explanation of fees – HUD-1, title insurance, pre-paids, escrow expenses, loan origination fees
4. Required closing documents
5. Funding – rescission periods

D. Financial Calculations

1. Periodic interest
2. Monthly payments
3. Down payments
4. Closing costs/prepaids
5. ARM adjustments – interest rates and payments

IV. Ethics (18%)   105

A. Ethical Issues

1. Prohibited acts:
    a) Redlining
    b) RESPA prohibitions
    c) Kickbacks/compensation
    d) Permitted/prohibited duties
2. Fairness in lending:
    a) Referral (Definition/required disclosures)
    b) Coercion
    c) Appraiser conflict of interest
    d) Discrimination/fairness
3. Fraud detection:
    a) Asset/income/employment fraud
    b) Sales contract/application red flags
    c) Occupancy fraud
    d) General red flags
4. Suspicious bank and other activity; information not provided to borrower; verifying application information
5. Advertising:
    a) Misleading information
    b) Due diligence review
    c) "Unfair, deceptive, or abusive acts"
    d) Federal regulation
6. Predatory lending and steering

B. Ethical behavior related to loan origination activities

1. Financial responsibility:
    a) Permitted fees/compensation; fee changes; closing cost scenarios; referral fees; fee splitting

2. Handling borrower complaints
3. Mortgage company compliance:
    a) Discovery of material information; information supplied by employers
4. Relationships with consumers:
    a) Handling personal information/cybersecurity; disclosing conflicts of interest; requesting credit reports
    b) Changes in down payments or offered interest rates; powers of attorney; non-resident coborrowers
    c) Unreported/fluctuating income; gifts/unexplained deposits; appraiser interactions; multiple applications
    d) Truth in marketing and advertising – permissible statements in advertising
    e) General business ethics:
        i. Falsified information by borrower or MLO
        ii. Giving solicited/unsolicited advice
        iii. Outside parties seeking information

Content Outline Study Guide

*Note: Due to copyright laws, we cannot provide exact language for codes and regulations in some cases. It is strongly recommended to review the listed sections for complete information along with this study guide. Links for the regulations and other helpful materials are found on the official NMLS Content Outline.

I. Federal Mortgage-related Laws (24%)

A. Real Estate Settlement Procedures Act (RESPA), 12 CFR Part 1024 (Regulation X)

    1. RESPA origins and purpose; definition of "mortgage broker"

RESPA stands for the Real Estate Settlement Procedures Act and is overseen by the Consumer Financial Protection Bureau (CFPB). RESPA was enacted in 1974 by Congress to help consumers to obtain costs for settlement services at closing so that they may have the ability to choose appropriately between loan providers. RESPA also includes provisions to protect consumers from high settlement costs or lenders who participate in prohibited acts such as kickbacks or referral fees.

The main purposes of RESPA include:

- To provide disclosures throughout the real estate process to help educate purchasers so that they may make better decisions and more easily understand the process and materials provided to them.
- To enact the prohibition of unlawful practices by real estate professionals such as kickbacks and referral fees.

RESPA requires disclosures to be provided to homebuyers at four different times during the homebuying process:

- The time of application
- Before settlement
- At settlement
- After Settlement

As per RESPA definitions section 1024.2, a mortgage broker is defined as the following:

"A person that performs origination services and acts as an intermediary between a borrower and a lender in a transaction involving a federally related mortgage loan."

2. Applicable loan types

RESPA covers any federally related mortgage loan such as:

- Most loans secured by a lien, whether it be a first or subordinate position on residential property
- Home purchase loans
- Lender approved assumptions
- Refinance loans
- Loans for property improvement
- Home equity lines of credit
- Reverse mortgages.

3. RESPA prohibitions, limitations, & exemptions

RESPA includes a number of prohibited practices for the protection of consumers. They include:

- Section 6: Right to proper servicing of the loan
- Section 8: Prohibiting a person from receiving anything of value for a referral of settlement services or being paid without performing a service.
- Section 9: Prohibits the requirement of settlement services from a particular company directly or indirectly
- Section 10: Limits the amount of money a lender may hold in escrow

To expand on each section:

- Section 6: This section covers consumer protections in regards to the servicing of their loans. One of the aspects is any "qualified written request" to a loan servicer concerning must be followed by a written acknowledgment within 20 business days of receipt of the request. Additionally, any corrections to the borrower's account must be made within 60 days.

- Section 8: Forbids anyone in a mortgage transaction from giving or accepting payment of any kind for referrals of settlement services. Additionally, a person cannot receive a portion of a charge for services that are not performed. These are also known as kickbacks, fee-splitting, and unearned fees. Any violations are subject to criminal and civil penalties, including a fine of up to $10,000 and one year in prison.

- Section 9: A home buyer cannot be forced to use settlement services from a particular company as a condition of sale. Legal action may be taken against a seller who violates this provision for an amount equal to three times all charges made for the title insurance.

- Section 10: Puts limitations on how much a borrower is required to hold in an escrow account for the payment of taxes, hazard insurance, and other charges. Lenders cannot impose an escrow account on borrowers except in the cases of government loan program requirements. The maximum a lender can require a borrower to put into an escrow account shall be no more than 1/12 of the total of all disbursements payable during the year, plus an amount necessary to pay for any shortage in the account. In addition, the lender may require a cushion to ensure that there is always enough for making payments. The maximum shall not exceed an amount equal to 1/6 of the total disbursements for the year. An escrow account analysis can be performed once during the year or at the borrower's request. The borrower must be notified of any shortage. If the analysis shows an excess in escrow of $50 or more, the amount must be returned to the borrower.

Section 1024.5 covers the applicability of RESPA. Most loans will need to comply with the requirements if they are federally related mortgages and don't meet any of the exemptions provided in (b) through (d) of the section. These exemptions include:

- Business purpose loans
- Temporary loans
- Loans for vacant lots
- Secondary market transactions
- Assumptions without lender approval
- Loan conversions

A lender may own or have a partial interest in real estate, mortgage or title companies. RESPA requires that when one of these entities refers the applicant to another affiliated provider, the loan applicant receives an Affiliated Business Arrangement Disclosure. This disclosure must include the details of the relationship and the estimate for the service. It shall be provided at the time of the referral and no later.

When an MLO is also the mortgage broker, a lender may choose not to separately disclose any credit or charge for the interest rate selected for the loan. In this scenario, the lender must disclose that the origination charge includes the credit or charge for the interest rate.

4. Settlement services

Settlement services are any services provided in connection with a prospective or actual real estate transaction. These include:

- Origination services
- Mortgage broker services
- Services related to processing or funding

- Title services
- Attorney fees
- Document preparation
- Credit report
- Inspections
- Use of a settlement agent
- Mortgage insurance
- Hazard or flood insurance
- Life or disability insurance
- Property taxes
- Agent or broker fees
- Any other settlement services

A loan originator must provide the borrower with a written list of settlement service providers at the time the loan estimate is provided. When the borrower decides to shop for and select the settlement service providers, the loan originator must indicate the settlement service and corresponding charge to be paid.

5. Required borrower information on application (Regulation X)

The borrower must include all of the basic information necessary to be considered for the loan. This includes:

- Name
- Social security
- Address
- Loan amount
- Income
- Property value

6. Foreclosure process

RESPA provides certain rights to the borrower in the case of an inability to make payments and the lender must follow a specific process. RESPA indicates that the first notice of default cannot be made unless one of the following is true:

- The borrower is 120 days delinquent on the mortgage loan obligation
- The foreclosure is based on the borrower's violation of a due-on-sale clause
- The servicer has joined the foreclosure action of a subordinate lienholder

The borrower may also submit a complete loss mitigation application during the pre-foreclosure period. This must be followed by a review and statement from the lender regarding loss mitigation before an official notice of foreclosure is provided.

The types of foreclosure include:

- Judicial foreclosure: The foreclosure procedure requires a court action or proceeding.
- Non-judicial foreclosure – recording or publication requirement: The foreclosure procedure does not require an action or court proceeding.
- Non-judicial foreclosure – no recording or publication requirement: The foreclosure procedure does not require an action or court proceeding and also does not require any document to be recorded or published.

Additionally, the lender and the borrower may agree to a short sale. This is when there is an agreement to sell the home, without going to auction, for less than the amount of the existing principal balance.

If the home goes to auction and is not sold, the property becomes seized by the lender and is classified as Real Estate Owned (REO)

7. Initial escrow statements

If an escrow account is required, the borrower must receive an initial escrow statement. This includes an itemization of all escrow related items including property taxes, hazard insurance, and PMI expected from the account within the first 12 months of the account. The statement shall be provided at closing or within 45 days of the establishment of the escrow account.

B. Equal Credit Opportunity Act (ECOA), 12 CFR Part 1002 (Regulation B)

1. ECOA permissible acts

The Federal Trade Commission (FTC) enforces the Equal Credit Opportunity Act (ECOA) which aims to prevent credit discrimination due to race, religion, nationality, gender, marital status, age, or receipt of public assistance. These factors may not be used for the determination of credit worthiness. There is information that is acceptable to be questioned under the act. These include:

- Immigration status
- Permanent residency
- Credit history
- May ask if a client is receiving child support or alimony

2. Factors that cannot be used to discriminate

The Equal Credit Opportunity Act prohibits discrimination in all aspects of the mortgage process on the basis of all of the following:

- Gender
- Marital status (unless in a community property state)
- Age
- Race
- Ethnicity
- Religion
- Nationality
- Receipt of public assistance

The terms which may be used to describe individuals in which marriage is involved are limited to married, unmarried, or separated.

Disparate treatment is the treatment of an individual worse than others based on a protected characteristic such as gender, race, religion, etc. This would be a male being given a lower interest rate than females of the same application status or similar.

3. Circumstances where a loan can be denied

Acceptable reasons are related to the applicant's inability to display creditworthiness but may also be related to the proposed property. Common circumstances for denial may include:

- Poor credit history
- Insufficient assets
- Proposed property having unfavorable characteristics
- Lack of employment history
- Poor credit score
- Immigration status

4. Regulation B

Regulation B was instituted to protect applicants from discrimination throughout the credit process. It provides requirements to lenders for compliance. They shall not discriminate based on age, gender, ethnicity, nationality, marital status, or income from public assistance.

The two main aspects of Regulation B include:

- A creditor shall not discriminate against an applicant regarding any aspect of a credit transaction.

- A creditor shall not make any oral or written statement, in advertising or otherwise, to applicants or prospective applicants that would discourage, on a prohibited basis, a reasonable person from making or pursuing an application.

5. Notifying borrower of action taken (timing)

Notice shall be provided within 30 days on an existing account. The notice should include a statement of specific reasons for the denial, including the credit agency which provided information credit information.

6. Required disclosures when application denied

If a lender chooses to deny a loan application, the consumer has certain rights to information that must be disclosed. These include:

- Reason for denial or informing the consumer that they have the right to request the reason for denial
- Notice of decision within 30 days of application
- Specific reasons for denial such as income or employment history
- Reasons for less favorable terms if offered
- Right to receive an appraisal if applicable
- Negative information from a credit report that influenced the decision

7. Adverse action: definition/examples/notifications/timing

Adverse action can be defined as a negative action taken on an account concerning the denial or altering of credit. It may include the refusal to grant credit in the amount or terms requested in an application which may include a counteroffer to the applicant.

Adverse action shall include all of the following:

- Reason for denial or action taken
- Name and address of creditor
- ECOA notice of prohibition against discrimination
- If the action taken was due to the credit history, then the credit reporting agency must be listed
- Credit information

As per Regulation B, notice is required when a creditor has taken adverse action for the following situations:

- A completed credit application

- An incomplete credit application
- An existing credit account

Additionally, notice shall be given if a borrower does not accept a counteroffer provided by a creditor.

Notice is not required if:

- No credit is involved in the transaction
- A counteroffer made by the creditor is accepted by the borrower
- The application is withdrawn
- The applicant fails to inquire within 30 days after application if there is an understanding by both parties that the applicant was committed to inquire

Situations of adverse action include:

- A creditor chooses not to provide credit in the amount or for the terms requested.
- Termination of an account
- A change in the terms that is unfavorable and does not affect the creditor's accounts
- A refusal to increase the amount of credit available to an applicant who has applied for an increase

Adverse action shall include a notice which details the reason for rejection. This helps to ensure there is no potential for rejection on the basis of discrimination. Any applicant that is denied based on their credit report is allowed by law to review the report without cost or penalty. Adverse actions are reported on an individual's credit report and shall be itemized for informational purposes.

8. Information required on the application; definition of "elderly"

Besides the information needed to evaluate the creditworthiness of an applicant, the following information shall be provided to ensure lenders may be properly monitored so as to not fail to comply with ECOA:

- Ethnicity
- Gender
- Race

The providing of this information is optional. If the applicant chooses not to, the lender must document this.

An applicant must be notified of an incomplete application within 30 days by a notice of incompleteness which indicates the required missing information and a deadline for submission. This must include a notice indicating that failure to provide the missing information will result in a discontinuation of consideration.

Section 1002.2(o) defines the age of an elderly person as 62.

9. Mortgage loan originator (MLO) actions when borrower refuses to provide race/gender information

If this information is not provided, the MLO shall indicate this by checking "Did not wish to furnish" on the application. Proper documentation of this ensures the compliance of the MLO

10. Co-signer requirements

The requirements for the cosigner must follow all of the restrictions of discrimination in regard to sex, marital status, race, and others. The creditor can however dictate certain stipulations such as the location of the cosigner in relation to the applicant. This is outlined in section 1002.7(d)(5).

11. Acceptable income for loan review

The ECOA requires the lender or mortgage broker to consider reliable sources of income such as part-time, pensions, alimony, social security, public assistance, and others. However, the applicant is not required to submit alimony, child support, or separate maintenance as income.

12. Creditworthiness factors

Regulation B does not have any specific guidance on methods of analyzing credit. Creditors may use methods based on judgment, or they may statistically develop techniques such as credit scoring.

Prohibitions of the evaluation of creditworthiness include:

- A creditor must not consider the potential for children affecting income
- Denying an applicant without a telephone listing
- A creditor may not discount or exclude part-time income from an applicant or the spouse of an applicant.

Credit risk is evaluated by five different characteristics, often referred to as the "5 C's" of creditworthiness:

- Credit history
- Capacity

- Capital
- Collateral
- Conditions

C. Truth in Lending Act (TILA), 12 CFR Part 1026 (Regulation Z)

<u>1. Purpose of TILA</u>

The Truth in Lending Act (TILA) of 1968 was created to guard consumers in transactions including lenders and creditors. TILA stipulates that certain information must be disclosed for an individual to receive credit. Some of the items include annual percentage rate (APR), loan term, and the total costs of borrowing the money. This information must be made clear on the documents necessary for obtaining the credit.

In addition to providing a uniform system for disclosures, the act:

- Protects consumers in the event of unfair credit billing and credit card practices
- Provides consumers with rescission rights
- Provides rate caps on certain dwelling-secured loans
- Imposes limitations on home equity lines of credit and certain closed-end home mortgages
- Provides minimum standards for most dwelling-secured loans
- Defines and prohibits unfair or deceptive mortgage lending practices.

The TILA and Regulation Z do not regulate how much interest a financial institution may charge or whether they shall provide a loan to a consumer.

<u>2. Loans covered under TILA</u>

The following criteria must apply for a loan to be subject to TILA:

- The loan must be primarily for personal use
- The loan must be for an individual, not a business
- The loan has a minimum of 4 installment payments

<u>3. Definitions including APR, finance charge, dwelling, residential mortgage loan</u>

The annual percentage rate (APR) is the total cost to the borrower for borrowing the principal. This includes the interest rate and any other costs associated with the loan. These include:

- Points
- Broker fees
- Closing costs

There is an acceptable change in APR that does not trigger the need to re-evaluate and initiate a new waiting period. The amount is 1/8th of a percent for fixed loans and 1/4th of a percent for adjustable-rate loans. This only applies to increases in the rate. A decrease in the rate does not initiate a new waiting period.

Not all fees are included in the calculation of the APR such as appraisal, credit reporting, or inspection fees. It is important for a consumer to understand what is included in the calculation of an APR.

A finance charge is any fee which represents the cost of borrowing or obtaining credit. This includes interest on the loan and any fees associated with obtaining the loan.

A dwelling refers to a residential structure which may include between 1 and 4 units.

A residential mortgage loan is a mortgage or equivalent consensual security interest for the consumer's principal dwelling or the construction of that dwelling.

Business days are any day except Sundays and Federal holidays. The holidays which are not considered business days are as detailed in 5 U.S.C 6103(a).

4. "Notice of right to rescind"; refinance rescind scenarios; defining "seller contributions"

The right to rescind is the ability of a borrower to cancel the proposed transaction and is covered in section 1026. There are specific disclosures and requirements related to the action. TILA section 1026.15(b) provides the requirements of notice and disclosures to the consumer for a right to rescind. The disclosures are as follows:

- "The retention or acquisition of a security interest in the consumer's principal dwelling.
- The consumer's right to rescind.
- How to exercise the right to rescind
- The effects of rescission.
- The date the rescission period expires."

In no way should there be a recommendation included with the required information.

As per section 1026.23(f):

"The right to rescind does not apply to refinancing transactions for a principal dwelling except to the extent the new amount financed exceeds the unpaid principal balance, any earned unpaid finance charge on the existing debt, and amounts attributed solely to the costs of the refinancing or consolidation."

Seller contributions may be used for closing costs, pre-paid costs, or discount points but not for down payment amounts. There are limits on seller contributions based on the loan type and the amount put down on the loan:

- Conventional loan primary residence
    - Less than 10% down: Maximum 3%
    - 10-25% down: 6% Max.
    - 25% or greater: 9% Max.
- Conventional Investment property: 2% Max.
- FHA loan: 6% Max.
- VA loan: 4% of the sale price plus reasonable and customary loan costs
- USDA loan: 6% Max.

5. Home Ownership and Equity Protection Act (HOEPA), high-cost mortgages (12 CFR 1026.32)

HOEPA was enacted to protect consumers involved in mortgages with high APRs or high points and fees. Practices which are prohibited under HOEPA include:

- Recommendation of a default on an existing loan to then be replaced by a high-cost mortgage
- Any fees to modify, renew, defer, amend, or extend a high-cost mortgage
- Maximum of 4% of the past due payments for late fees
- The ballooning of late fees
- Fees for generating payoff statements are not allowed
- Points and fees cannot be financed
- By law, a loan structure created with the intent to circumvent HOEPA is prohibited

HOEPA is enforced by the Consumer Financial Protection Bureau (CFPB).

The Home Ownership and Equity Protection Act includes four types of transactions:

- Purchase-money mortgages
- Refinances
- Closed-end home equity loan
- Open-end credit plans

Covered loans are those which meet the following criteria:

- An original mortgage that has an APR of 8 points or more than the treasury security rate.
- A second mortgage that has an APR 10 points or more than the treasury security rate.
- The total amount payable to the lender before closing including fees and points is greater than 8% of the loan amount

HOEPA prohibits compensation programs based on the terms or conditions of a mortgage. Brokers shall not originate loans with higher interest rates and undesirable terms to receive higher compensation. They are also prohibited from dual compensation. Brokers shall also not persuade or steer borrowers to use specific products which may increase the compensation.

6. Higher-priced mortgage loans (12 CFR 1026.35)

High-priced mortgages are those which for a first-lien mortgage has an APR that exceeds the APOR by 1.5 percent or more. For a subordinate mortgage, a loan is high-priced if its APR exceeds the APOR by 3.5 percent.

High priced mortgages shall not include:

- HELOC's
- Reverse mortgages
- Construction only loans
- Temporary or bridge loans with terms less than 12 months

There are restrictions on the refinancing of high-priced mortgages in which they shall not result in a higher balance, balloon payment or negative amortization.

7. MLO compensation (12 CFR 1026.36(d))

This section provides prohibitions on a company's compensation to the mortgage broker. It states that a loan originator shall not receive compensation in an amount that is based on the following:

- Transaction term
- The terms of multiple transactions by an individual loan originator, or
- The terms of multiple transactions by multiple individual loan originators.

The following are acceptable means of compensation:

- The loan originator's overall dollar volume delivered to the creditor
- The long-term performance of the originator's loans.
- A determined hourly rate
- A payment that is fixed in advance

- Based on a percentage of applications submitted by the loan originator to the creditor that results in consummated transactions.

Compensation rules indicate that:

- A loan originator shall not take direct or indirect compensation from anyone except the consumer involved in the transaction

- No one aware of the loan shall pay any compensation to a loan originator in connection with the transaction except the consumer.

D. TILA-RESPA Integrated Disclosure Rule (TRID) ("Know Before You Owe")

<u>1. Purpose of TRID</u>

The integrated disclosure rule was meant to try to simplify and streamline the mortgage process for applicants. This was made in an effort to reduce confusion that was found to be common in many mortgage transactions. Some main changes to the rule include replacing the good faith estimate with the loan estimate and the final HUD-1 form with the closing disclosure. TRID applies to most closed-end mortgages and does not apply to HELOCs, reverse mortgages, and a dwelling not attached to a real property.

TRID was introduced to reduce the amount of paperwork involved in mortgage transactions and to provide more clarity, understanding, and accuracy for the borrower. The goal of the act was also to reduce confusion. The required disclosures include:

- Loan Estimate – A loan estimate replaces the Good Faith Estimate (GFE). A loan estimate will be standardized with all lenders and will clearly state the terms and estimated fees. This will make shopping for a mortgage and comparing loan offers easier for consumers.
- Closing Disclosure – The HUD-1 statement has been replaced with the closing disclosure. The CD is implemented to make the costs and fees clear. The CD provides the actual costs at closing but can vary from the loan estimate within certain limitations.

<u>2. Loans covered under TRID</u>

Most closed-end loans which are secured by a property are covered by TILA with some exceptions. These exceptions include:

- Reverse mortgages
- HELOC's
- Loans secured by a home that is not attached to a property (ie. mobile home)
- Loans made by an entity which provides 5 or fewer mortgages in a calendar year

3. Loan estimates: facts, required information, charges/fees

The loan estimate is the initial form received after the application is received. It must be provided within 3 business days after receipt of the application. The information provided includes a best estimate of the interest rate, monthly payment, and closing costs for the loan. Also included will be anticipated property taxes and insurance costs.

The loan estimate shall also include any features of the loan including prepayment penalties or negative amortization. The loan estimate is not an indication of approval.

The loan estimate expires 10 days after issuing. Expiration of the loan estimate is considered a change in circumstance, and any further progress would require a revised LE.

Charges and fees disclosed on a loan estimate are divided into sections, including:

- Origination charges
- Fees that can be shopped for
- Fees that cannot be shopped for
- Taxes and government fees
- Prepaids
- Initial escrow costs
- Any other costs specific to the loan

Estimated information included in the loan estimate contains among others:

- Interest rate
- Monthly payment
- Total closing costs
- Prepayment penalties
- Amounts that can increase after closing
- Mortgage insurance
- End of mortgage insurance
- Loan costs
- Prepaids
- Taxes
- Cash to close

If a professional refers a business in connection with a real estate transaction, has an ownership in a business that can be used as a service, or can in any way influence the selection of specific service, a disclosure of affiliated business must be provided. This disclosure must include the details of the relationship and the estimate for the service. It shall be provided at the time of the referral and no later.

The loan estimate is ultimately the responsibility of the creditor to be provided to the consumer. There are situations where a mortgage broker may provide the LE upon receipt of the application, but it is the creditor's responsibility to ensure its compliance with requirements.

4. Definition of "loan consummation"

Loan consummation is the time at which the borrower becomes contractually obligated to meet the agreement of the loan terms to the creditor. This is not necessarily the same as closing or settlement, as different states may have different laws regarding when the obligation is final.

5. Special information booklet

The special information booklet also called the settlement costs booklet, is a part of the required disclosures to the applicant at the time of the loan application. It is an informational booklet that can help borrowers become familiar with the home-buying and mortgage process. The goal of the booklet is to help promote informed decisions and avoid common pitfalls. It includes:

- Steps in buying a home
- Mortgage process
- Fees
- Disclosures

The exceptions for providing the special information pamphlet are in section 1024.6(a)(3) and are:

- Refinance
- Closed-end loans
- Reverse mortgages
- Any other federally related mortgage loan whose purpose is not the purchase of a 1-4 family residential property

6. Closing Disclosure

Closing disclosure provides the final costs and specifications of the loan. The information provided includes:

- Final interest rate
- Monthly payment

- Closing costs
- Cash to close
- Prepayment penalty
- Costs that may increase after closing
- Breakdown of closing costs
- Total cost of the loan
- APR
- Total interest paid over the life of the loan
- Late payment penalties
- Indication of negative amortization
- Loan assumption indication

7. Disclosures timing

The closing disclosure must be provided 3 days prior to loan consummation. The date at which it must be provided also depends on the method of delivery as email and hand-delivered methods begin the timeline immediately, but mail has an additional time to allow for delivery. The 3-days does not include Sundays and Federal holidays.

The loan estimate shall be provided no more than 3 days after the mortgage application and no less than 7 days prior to loan consummation. A revised loan estimate must be provided within 3 days of the newly discovered or altered information and no less than 4 days prior to consummation.

The closing disclosure is required no less than 3 days prior to loan consummation.

8. MLO actions if TRID disclosure is incomplete

Upon recognition of incomplete information on a loan estimate, the missing items must be requested and provided immediately.

9. "Change of circumstances"

A loan estimate may be amended only for specific situations. These include:

- Changed circumstances including new information or an event outside of the control of all parties involved
- When a floating rate is subsequently locked
- Expiration of the LE
- When a financial institution chooses to provide a courtesy LE

There are three types of events that qualify for a change in circumstance:

- An extraordinary event beyond the control of anyone involved in the transaction, such as a natural disaster.
- Information that the lender relied upon to make a decision has changed.
- The discovery of new information which may affect the lender's decisions.

10. Information that must be provided to consumer upon request

If the consumer requests a change that has an effect on the established loan estimate, the results of that change must be disclosed as a part of a revised loan estimate as well as with the impact of the change.

11. Borrower's right to rescission

The right to rescission is the borrower's ability to cancel a loan on a "no questions asked basis" for a minimum period after closing. This applies only to refinancing and home equity loans, not to purchase loans. A borrower has a rescission period of 3 business days.

12. Annual escrow statement

The annual escrow statement is an evaluation of the status of the escrow account for a mortgage. The monthly payments required for property taxes and insurance are an estimate of the actual yearly bill. It is common for these bills to increase or decrease in which case there needs to be a reassessment of the monthly payments for the following year to ensure there are sufficient funds at the time of payment due. The reassessment may result in an increase or decrease in the monthly obligations.

E. Other Federal Laws and Guidelines

1. Home Mortgage Disclosure Act (HMDA), 12 CFR Part 1003 (Regulation C)

a. Mortgages in reportable data

The Home Mortgage Disclosure Act applies to residential loans including:

- Purchase
- Refinance
- Home improvement
- Subordinate financing

It does not apply to the purchase of vacant land or a construction loan

b. HMDA definition of "dwelling"

As per HMDA section 1003.2(f), a dwelling is not limited to the principal residence and can also be:

- Second-home
- Multifamily residential structure
- Mixed-use properties
- Properties with service and medical uses

Structures not attached to properties such as mobile homes and boats are not included in the dwelling definition. Also excluded are transitionary homes such as dormitories, hospitals, and hotels.

c. Information included in borrower data

Borrower data covers the pertinent information to the applicant and the loan, such as:

- Ethnicity
- Race
- Sex
- Loan type
- Loan amount
- Loan status
- Income
- Assets

d. Information that a borrower must include on an application

An application must consist of the following six pieces of information:

- Name
- Income
- Social Security
- Property address
- Estimate of the property value
- Desired loan amount

e. Information about which an MLO should not inquire

The originator must not ask directly about any demographic data related to the applicant. The opportunity to provide this information shall be included to applicants by indicating that they may select their race on the application and are able to select more than one category for race.

It must be made known to the applicant that the demographic data is used solely to monitor and enforce compliance with fair lending laws.

f. Information provided by the borrower regarding the right of refusal

The applicant must be given the ability not to provide certain personal data. The originator shall indicate that this has been chosen when providing the application for documentation purposes to ensure the law has been complied with.

2. Fair Credit Reporting Act (FCRA)/Fair and Accurate Credit Transactions Act (FACTA) 15 USC §1681 et seq.

a. Definition of a "fraud alert"

A fraud alert is a notice on a credit report that indicates that the consumer may have been a victim of identity theft. This provides protection to the consumer so that they may not be denied a loan for reasons of fraud.

b. Information included in a "consumer report"

A consumer report is provided by credit agencies and includes information about the applicant. It may include:

- Creditworthiness
- Credit standing
- Credit capacity
- Character
- General reputation
- Personal characteristics
- Mode of living

c. Permissible times when a credit report may be accessed

FCRA provides limitations on when a credit report can be accessed without written consent from the consumer. These include those who have a current or potential relationship with the consumer such as a landlord, utility company, employer, or insurance company. FCRA also provides other instances where it is permissible for credit to be pulled:

- When credit is applied for
- Application for insurance
- When a creditor intends to extend credit
- Employment related scenarios with the consent of the applicant

- Court ordered
- Government benefits or licensure applications
- Any "legitimate business need" for a business transaction

d. Requirement to develop policies and procedures regarding identity theft

Financial institutions involved in credit transactions must establish procedures for the prevention of identity theft. Each program must satisfy the following requirements:

- Identify relevant patterns, practices, and specific forms of activity that are red flags. These red flags shall signal possible identity theft.
- Detect red flags.
- Respond promptly and in a proper manner to any red flags
- Update the program on a regular basis in response to previous incidents.

e. Definition of "creditor"

A creditor is any entity that regularly extends, renews, or continues credit.

f. Information included in a FACTA disclosure

FACTA provides requirements for how the information provided by consumers can be shared. The consumer shall be informed that:

- The three major credit reporting agencies shall provide a consumer's credit score without charge.
- Consumers can place an alert on their profile to indicate the potential for being a victim of fraud.
- The consumer's personal account numbers shall not be made fully visible.

g. Length of time a bankruptcy will show on a credit history

For a chapter 13 bankruptcy, the length of time is 7 years. For chapter 7, it is 10 years.

h. Credit score evaluation methods

There are three credit agencies which report a score indicating the creditworthiness of a consumer. The three are Experian, Equifax, and Transunion. The score has a range from 300 to 850.

3. Federal Trade Commission Red Flag rules, 16 CFR Part 681

a. Parties subject to "red flag" rules

Not all creditors are subject to the "red flag" rule. A business has to evaluate if the following scenarios apply:

- Is there a deferred payment for goods and services or bill customers?
- Do they grant or arrange credit?
- Do they participate in the decision to extend, renew, or set the terms of credit?

b. Enforcement authority for "red flag" rules

Enforcement of the red flag rules is determined by the Federal Trade Commission (FTC)

4. Bank Secrecy Act/Anti-money Laundering (BSA/AML)

a. Requirement that companies protect consumer information

Financial institutions are required to take steps to protect the privacy of consumers' finances under federal law. The FTC is one of the federal agencies that enforce the law which covers banks, securities firms, insurance companies, and companies providing financial products and services. Agencies are subject to the Financial Privacy Rule, which governs how financial institutions can collect and disclose customers' personal financial information, and the Safeguards Rule, which requires all financial institutions to maintain safeguards to protect customer information. Institutions are also prohibited from pretexting which is when companies gain access to consumers' personal financial information under false pretenses.

b. Facts about Suspicious Activity Reports (SARs)

If a financial institution suspects suspicious or illegal behavior, they must file a Suspicious Activity Report (SAR). The report must be filed no more than 30 days after the initial detection of the violation. Associated documentation and the report must be kept for 5 years by the financial institutions. The person being investigated shall not be told about the report.

c. Circumstances that require filing a SAR

The primary goal of filing a suspicious activity report and the ensuing investigation is to prevent the following:

- Money laundering
- Fraud
- Terrorist funding

There are specific minimums for the dollar amount of the violation for when there is a requirement to file:

- Criminal violations involving insider abuse in any amount.
- Criminal violations of $5,000 or more when a suspect can be identified.
- Criminal violations of $25,000 or more regardless of a potential suspect.
- Transactions through the bank or any affiliate aggregating $5,000 or more, if there is suspicion of any of the following:
    - Potential money laundering or other illegal activity.
    - Intent to evade the BSA
    - A transaction with no identifiable purpose
    - A transaction that is outside of what is normally expected

d. SAR privacy requirements

The institution filing the SAR shall not tell the individual being investigated that they are being investigated. Access to the information shall only be provided to necessary parties to the investigation such as the FBI.

5. Gramm-Leach-Bliley Act (GLBA) – Privacy, Federal Trade Commission Safeguard Rules and DoNot-Call

a. Non-public information regarding a customer

Non-public information can be classified as any personally identifiable information provided by a consumer to a financial institution in connection with obtaining a financial product or service. The GLBA protects the distribution of such information in unacceptable ways.

b. Permissible use of non-public information regarding a customer

The GLBA provides guidance to institutions regarding the sharing of non-public information. They must at a minimum disclose:

- What information is collected about its customers
- With whom the financial institution shares the information
- How the information is protected
- Opt-out options

c. Purpose of act

The GLBA protects the consumer's personal financial information and requires financial institutions to explain how they will share and protect this private information. This includes a disclosure of policies to the consumer related to these processes. The GLBA contains three main provisions:

- Privacy rule
- Safeguard rule
- Pre-texting rule

d. Requirement for written privacy policy disclosures

The Act requires a financial institution to notify the consumer if they plan to share personal information with any third parties. The consumer must be supplied with both a privacy notice and an opt-out notice. The privacy notice must contain the institution's policy on the sharing of information and the types of information shared. This must be provided no later than the time the relationship is established with the consumer. An annual notice must also be provided but it is acceptable to be posted online and not directly distributed.

e. Acceptable delivery methods for a privacy notice

The privacy notice must be delivered in written form unless specifically requested with written notice to be provided electronically from the consumer.

f. Permissible hours for telephone calls

Permissible hours include 8 AM to 9 PM.

g. Written policies for maintaining do-not-call lists

Entities making calls must maintain written policies that shall be provided on demand. The person making the calls must be trained and informed of the existence of the do-not-call list. Requests from consumers to not receive calls must be internally recorded, including the name and telephone number of the person.

h. Precautions to protect customer information

The act provides protections to the consumer which will allow for the protection of non-public information. These include:

- Providing initial privacy notice
- Opt-out notice
- Annual privacy notice
- Prohibitions of sharing information for marketing purposes

i. Purpose of the National Do-Not-Call Registry

The do-not-call registry protects consumers from unwanted solicitations on the phone. It is managed and maintained by the Federal Trade Commission (FTC). Those who choose to be on the list will limit but not eliminate any telemarketing calls from personal information. Telemarketers are required to check the list no less than once every 31 days. A consumer who is called impermissibly may file a complaint with the FTC and a penalty of up to $16,000 per incident is possible.

j. Permissible solicitation scenarios

The do-not-call register does not eliminate all scenarios for telemarketing. There are situations where a business is exempt from the restrictions, such as:

- Charities or non-profits
- A telemarketing business who has an existing relationship with a consumer may continue to call for 18 months.
- Survey calls or political polls
- Caller with written permission from a specific consumer
- An organization that makes only business-to-business calls

k. Do-not-call request

Consumers are able to join the list online for free by adding their telephone number to the database. They may also do so over the phone by the number provided by the FTC.

l. Retention of information after a solicitation

Information acquired after a solicitation can be retained for 2 years.

6. Mortgage Acts and Practices – Advertising, 12 CFR Part 1014 (Regulation N)

a. Advertisements referring to specific credit terms

Advertisements which refer to specific terms must be clear and concise and disclose:

- APR
- Terms of repayment
- Amount of down payment

b. Length of time required to retain advertisements

Entities which are subject to the act must maintain records for 24 months from the last date of any commercial communication regarding any mortgage product.

c. Information required to be included in an advertisement

If an advertisement includes any type of credit, it must include terms that are actually and readily available to the public. Misrepresentations of actually available terms are prohibited.

d. Triggering terms that require additional disclosure

Triggering terms are those which when used require additional information to be provided. Triggering terms are outlined in section 1026.24(d)(1) include:

- A down payment (percentage or amount)
- The number of payments
- The loan term
- A finance charge

Any mentioning of these terms must include as appropriate the following:

- Amount or % of the down payment
- Terms of repayment
- Use of the term "annual percentage rate" and if the rate may be increased

e. Violations of the act

The act prohibits misrepresentations or misleading claims in advertising. As per section 1014.3, this includes among others:

- Type and amount of mortgage fees
- Terms, payments, or amount of loan
- Taxes or insurance associated with a loan
- Type of mortgage
- Interest rate details
- Misrepresentations of the source of commercial communication
- The ability of a consumer to be approved for a loan

7. Electronic Signatures in Global and National Commerce Act (E-Sign Act)

a. Required E-Sign disclosures

Prior to obtaining consumer consent for an e-signature, the lender must provide the following:

- The right to have the required documents provided in paper format.
- The right to withdraw consent and any associated stipulations associated with withdrawal.
- Whether the consent applies to a specific transaction or others as well.
- Procedures for withdrawal of consent.
- Hardware and software requirements for e-signature.

b. Borrower's consent regarding access to information in electronic format

For the documents and communication to be provided electronically, the borrower must be provided and sign an E-Sign Act Disclosure and Electronic Consent form. This notifies the borrower of their right to choose to receive communication and documents electronically. For this to occur, the lender must follow the following process:

- Inform the borrower of the availability of paper documents
- Inform the consumer of consent choices
- Disclose procedures to withdraw consent
- Provide hardware and software requirements
- Obtain affirmative consent
- Provide disclosure of any changes after consent

c. Requirements for maintaining records in electronic format

There are no specific timeframes for the requirement of electronic record retention outside of those for normal records, but the lender must maintain electronic records accurately and so that they may be provided to those who are allowed access. A single authoritative copy shall be kept for any purposes.

d. Ways to verify a borrower's identity

A financial institution must pursue the authentication of an individual seeking a mortgage. An individual's identity must be confirmed before proceeding with a mortgage loan. This is done by matching the information from the applicant with that of an independent source. Independent sources include, but are not limited to:

- National commercial credit bureaus
- Commercially available data sources or services

- State motor vehicle agencies
- Government databases

The minimum verification requirement is the name, date of birth, and either the social security number or driver's license number oof the applicant.

8. USA PATRIOT Act

a. Primary purpose of the act

The Patriot Act was established to monitor and deter terrorist acts and money laundering related to terrorism in the United States.

b. Major functions of the act

The act monitors, identifies, and reports suspicious activity on laundering and financial crimes related to terrorism. Some of the functions include:

- Lowers reportable receipt of money to $5,000
- Use of Suspicious Activity Reports
- Anti-Money Laundering
- Consumer Identification Program

c. Confidential nature of filing reports

All filing of complaints and concerns is confidential and can be done by filing a Suspicious Activity Report or over the phone for immediate attention.

d. Ways to verify a borrower's identity

The Customer Identification Program (CIP) requires financial institutions to have a policy in place to identify consumers. At a minimum a bank must obtain:

- Name
- Address
- Date of birth
- An assigned identification number

Verification can occur through documents or nondocumentary methods. A bank must have procedures in place for acceptable documentation of identity. They must provide the consumer's residence or nationality and photo identification at a minimum. Examples include driver's licenses and passports. Often times banks will require two forms of identification. Nondocumentary methods may include:

- Consumer interview
- Independent verification through comparisons to other databases
- Checking references such as other financial institutions

e. Parties subject to the act

Those subject to the act include:

- Federally regulated banks
- Foreign banks with locations in the United States
- Any persons involved in real estate transactions
- Non-federally regulated private banks
- Finance companies

f. Requirement to have a customer identification program in place and verification of the identities of borrowers

The Patriot Act at a minimum requires a financial institution to comply with three procedures in regard to identity verification. As per section 326, they are:

- Verify a consumer's identity to a reasonable extent
- Maintain records used for identity verification
- Consult known lists of terrorists and criminals when evaluating any applicant

9. Homeowners' Protection Act (Private Mortgage Insurance (PMI) Cancellation Act)

a. Major functions of the act

This act was established as protection for consumers against overpayment of private mortgage insurance (PMI). Its main functions include:

- Establishing when homeowners can cancel or stop PMI payments
- Enforcing when lenders must stop charging for PMI
- Establishing required disclosures to the consumer from the lender
- Handling of unearned premiums that homeowners may pay

b. Documents that must be provided to a borrower at loan consummation

The HPA requires lenders to inform the consumer about their rights in regard to the removal or cancelation of PMI. The disclosures shall include:

- Amortization schedule including the point of removal for PMI

- When the consumer may request cancellation
- Any features of the loan that limit when the PMI may be removed

10. Dodd-Frank Act

a. Re-financing situations

The Dodd-Frank act limits lenders from allowing risky refinancing situations ensuring the consumer is able to repay the loan.

b. Law oversight over TRID

As a part of the Dodd-Frank Act, the CFPB was directed to integrate the TILA and RESPA into the TRID to simplify and clarify the mortgage process to consumers.

F. Regulatory Authority

1. Consumer Financial Protection Bureau (CFPB)

The Consumer Financial Protection Bureau aims to support, educate, and protect consumers seeking and using loans. The protection extends beyond mortgages and includes car, student, and others as well. The CFPB provides tools and examples to consumers as they progress through the loan process so that they may make informed decisions.

The CFPB also protects consumers by taking action against those who participate in illegal or predatory practices. Complaints can be filed, and companies are required to cooperate and respond.

The CFPB is also subject to the laws governing federal agencies to ensure they proceed in a fair and responsible manner. They have accountability to the President and Congress including annual reports, audits, and semi-annual testifying to Congress. The CFPB is also subject to veto by the Federal Stability Oversight Council (FSOC) and must consult with federal banking agencies when establishing new rules. There are a number of checks and balances towards the CFPB including a capped budget, small business rule processes, mandatory cost-benefit analyses, and mandatory stakeholder involvement and comment.

CFPB has oversight over a large number of entities to ensure enforcement of federal consumer finance laws. It has authority over banks, thrifts, and credit unions with assets over $10 Billion and any affiliates. Also, CFPB oversees non-bank mortgage originators and servicers, payday lenders, and private student lenders of any size. CFPB also maintains a list of depository institutions and affiliates.

The CFPB allows consumers to submit complaints if they believe a violation has occurred. Complaints are submitted online or over the phone. Complaints are then submitted to the company in question for a response. Complaints are published with personal information removed for the education of the public.

2. Department of Housing and Urban Development (HUD)

The Department of Housing and Urban Development (HUD) oversees federal programs that address issues for Americans seeking housing. HUD's goals are to increase homeownership, support community development, and increase access to affordable housing free from discrimination. The agency enforces federal housing laws, operates mortgage-supportive initiatives, and distributes millions of dollars in federal grants. It is divided into a number of offices including:

- Federal Housing Administration (FHA)
- Office of Public and Indian Housing
- Office of Community Planning and Development
- Office of Healthy Homes and Lead Hazard Control
- Office of Federal Housing Enterprise Oversight
- Office of Policy Development and Research
- Office of Fair Housing and Equal Opportunity
- Government National Mortgage Association (GNMA)

The primary programs administered by HUD include:

- Federal Housing Administration mortgage and loan insurance
- Community Development Block Grants for economic development, job opportunities and housing rehabilitation
- Rental assistance in the form of Section 8 certificates or vouchers for low-income households
- Fair housing public education and enforcement

Housing counselors can be used to provide advice on buying a home, renting, defaults, foreclosures, and credit issues. The Dodd-Frank Wall Street Reform and Consumer Protection Act included a requirement that mortgage lenders provide applicants with a list of local housing counselors. Lenders may fulfill the requirement in two ways:

- CFPB-developed housing counseling lists
- Generation of their own lists using the same HUD data that the CFPB uses.

Lenders are required to provide applicants for a Federally regulated loan with a list of counseling agencies that may be used for the purposes of guidance.

A lender may not issue a high-cost loan without receiving written certification that a borrower has received counseling from a certified counselor.

HUD is a cabinet-level agency that oversees a number of programs:

- FHA
- Office of Public and Indian Housing
- Office of Community Planning and Development
- Office of Healthy Homes and Lead Hazard Control
- Office of Federal Housing Enterprise Oversight
- Government National Mortgage Association
- Office of Fair Housing and Equal Opportunity

The Fair Housing Act protects people from discrimination for any home-buying related activities. The following are prohibitions for the protection of consumers:

It is illegal to take any of the following actions because of race, color, religion, sex, disability, familial status, or national origin for the sale of a property:

- Refusal to rent, sell, negotiate or make housing available
- Set different terms, conditions or privileges
- Provide a person with different housing services or facilities
- Falsely deny that housing is available for inspection, sale or rental
- Advertising must not indicate preference of any kind
- Impose different sales prices or rental charges
- Use of different qualification criteria
- Eviction
- Harassment
- Fail to complete or delay maintenance or repairs
- Push or recommend an individual to a particular building or neighborhood.
- Persuade or attempt to influence a homeowner to sell their homes by suggesting that people of a particular protected characteristic are about to move into the neighborhood. This practice is also known as blockbusting
- Deny membership to any related organizations

Similarly, the following is prohibited from discrimination in lending practices:

- Refusal to provide a mortgage loan

- Refusal to provide information regarding loans
- Impose different terms or conditions on a loan
- Appraisal discrimination
- Refusal to purchase a loan

The specific exemptions to the Fair Housing Act are:

- Rental of a room in a dwelling with no more than four independent units if the owner lives in one of the units
- Housing operated by private organizations or clubs which restrict membership
- Single-family purchase without a mortgage broker

II. Uniform State Content (11%)

A. SAFE Act and CSBS/AARMR Model State Law

1. SAFE Act:

a) General purpose and scope

The Nationwide Mortgage Licensing System (NMLS) is the web-based platform for the administration of licenses and compliance with federal requirements for professionals in the industry. They service mortgage lenders, originators, money transmitters, and money services looking to apply, renew, or maintain their licenses. The online service creates a uniform process for each state. NMLS makes state-specific applications easier by providing checklists for all requirements.

The NMLS SAFE Act also referred to as simply "The Act" prohibits individuals from engaging in residential mortgage lending services without complying with licensing requirements. This includes applying for, obtaining, and maintaining a license. The ACT's main objectives include:

- Accountability and tracking of MLO's to ensure a minimum level of competency
- Ensuring appropriate consumer protections
- Providing consumers with accessible and free information regarding the status of MLO's

b) Documents to be filed for public record

NMLS provides public access to the Registry which includes all information relating to the employment history and publicly adjudicated disciplinary and enforcement actions against, mortgage loan originators.

2. State Mortgage Regulatory Agencies:

a) Regulatory powers and responsibilities

The Federal government has regulatory authority over mortgage lenders and practices through the various agencies and Congressional Acts as described in this manual including TILA, RESPA, and the Dodd-Frank Act. In addition to all Federal regulations, each state has individual regulators. State regulators assist in the oversight of banking and compliance with state and federal laws and may impose additional state-specific requirements.

State regulators monitor, review, and oversee the actions of how those involved in the mortgage industry conduct business. Their responsibilities include:

- Consumer protection
- Investigations of allegations
- Audit
- Enforcement of legal action

The responsibilities of the state regulatory agencies include:

- Providing consumer complaint process
- Provide guidance for lenders and borrowers on the requirements of the mortgage process
- Implement regulations for consistency across the industry
- Enforce lender compliance with federal and state regulations

b) NMLS Registry and relationship with state regulators

The NMLS Federal Registry was created to fulfill the CFPB requirement for registration of federally chartered or insured institutions and their mortgage loan originators. It creates a system of identification and tracking for the purposes of compliance and examination. MLO's must be aware of their registration status and fulfill requirements to ensure they are properly licensed.

c) Frequency of exams

The frequency of examination for institutions is evaluated and determined by CFPB based on two considerations:

- An assessment of risk to consumers
- Ensuring consistency with statutory requirements

Advanced notice of upcoming examinations is be provided to supervised entities

d) MLO unique identifiers

Each institution or individual who is registered with the NMLS is assigned a specific number called a unique identifier. Its purpose is to ease the ability of supervision, compliance, and transparency by being able to track activities for specific companies or people. This also allows for uniformity of tracking across states and over time. The type of unique identifier is separated by:

- Companies: MU1
- People: MU2 or MU4
- Branches: MU3

e) CFPB authority and CFPB Loan Originator rule (dual compensation)

CFPB has the authority to conduct examinations of supervised entities to ensure compliance with Federal Regulations. The Supervision and Examination manual is used as a guideline to ensure compliance. The manual provides:

- Overview of the examination process
- Examination procedures including:
    - Compliance management system
    - Product-based procedures
    - Statutory and regulation-based procedures
- Templates for examination

Penalties are divided into three tiers with maximums as follows:

- Tier 1; Maximum: $5,437
- Tier 2 which includes recklessness; Maximum: $27,186
- Tier 3 which includes knowingly committing an act; Maximum: $1,087,450

The CFPB Loan Originator rule establishes regulations for how a mortgage loan originator in most closed-end mortgages shall be compensated. Some of the purposes of the rule include:

- Prohibiting compensation from being based on the terms of the transaction or a proxy for a transaction term
- Permitting methods of compensating loan originators such as bonuses, retirement plans, and others based on mortgage-related profits
- Prohibiting loan origination compensation from two parties such as the consumer and a creditor

3. License Law and Regulation:

a) People required to be licensed

Specific activities must be performed by a licensed individual. This is generally described as doing work which is in the business of loan origination.

b) MLO-licensed services

Some of the activities that must be performed by a licensed MLO include:

- Accepting residential mortgage loan applications
- Involvement in the negotiation of the terms of a residential mortgage loan
- Advertise the acceptance of mortgage loan application

c) Allowable activities by underwriters, clerical staff, and loan processors

The mortgage underwriter is responsible for approving or disapproving a loan application. The underwriter evaluates and verifies the applications and determines the applicants have the ability to repay the loan. Duties include:

- Approve or deny mortgage loan applications.
- Verifies employment, income, credit history, assets, and liabilities.
- They ensure that the specifications of a property and the terms of loans meet the financial institution's requirements and the applicable government regulations.
- Document the reasons for the approval or disapproval of loans.

The duties related to mortgage processes or underwriting for the receipt, collection, or distribution of information fall under administrative or clerical tasks. This also includes communication with a consumer for the purposes of obtaining information for the processing of a loan application.

Mortgage loan processors are responsible for facilitating the successful processing of a loan application. Responsibilities Include:

- Performing an initial assessment of potential borrowers by thoroughly examining their applications
- Assessing the credit standings of applicants through background research
- Interviewing applicants to evaluate their eligibility for a loan or mortgage
- Correspondence with applicants
- Records filing and retention

d) Entities requiring licensed MLO

Any entities which engage in the practices of mortgage loan lending activities must employ a licensed loan originator to properly administer the process.

e) Businesses not required to be licensed (depository institutions)

Loan officers at banks, credit unions, or mortgage companies owned by banks are only required to be registered and do not have to meet the same licensing requirements. Individual companies may have training requirements, but it is not mandated by federal law.

Businesses and individuals are not required to be licensed under the Federal SAFE Act simply for working for a mortgage company. The requirement comes for performing origination activities. Jobs that do not require a license include processors, underwriters, and assistants who are not involved in offering or negotiating loans. These requirements however are subject to individual state law.

The state may determine that an MLO license is not required for those in a nonprofit housing organization or counseling agencies. For this to be applicable, the lending or counseling activities must: "not meet the commercial context connotations of the compensation and gain requirements for licensure or that such activities are performed in an ancillary manner which does not merit a licensing requirement."

Not all federal regulations apply to business purpose loans. TILA and Regulation Z does not apply to loans made primarily for business or commercial purposes. To determine whether a loan has a business or a consumer purpose, the Official Commentary to Regulation Z has a five-factor test:

- The level of the relationship between the borrower's primary occupation and the acquisition.
- Involvement of the borrower in the transaction
- The ratio of total income from the acquisition to the total income of the borrower. A higher ratio indicates a more business-type relationship
- The larger the transaction, the more likely it is to be business purpose
- The borrower's purpose for the loan

RESPA and Regulation X specifically exempt loans made primarily for a business or commercial purpose and rely upon the definitions and guidelines set forth in Regulation Z for purposes of this determination.

f) Licensee qualifications & application process:

i. Pre-license education

Pre-licensure education is 20 hours minimum and must be approved by NMLS. The education shall include:

- 3 hours of federal law and regulations
- 3 hours of ethics
- 2 hours of standards on non-traditional mortgage lending

ii. Background checks

Prior to licensure and registration with the NMLS, mortgage loan originators must complete a criminal background check (CBC). To perform the check, a fingerprint must be provided and put on file. The results are provided to the employer upon completion. A new CBC must be completed for any change in employment.

iii. Other requirements

Mortgage loan originators must comply with the following to become licensed:

- Provide authorization for NMLS to pull a credit report
- Provide fingerprints for a criminal background check
- Input and maintain their own record in the NMLS Registry
- Pass the National Mortgage exam
- Take the 20 hours of pre-licensing education courses

iv. Felony charges

There are strict limitations for felonies and licensure. A part of the minimum requirements for MLO's includes not having a felony in the past seven years. Felonies specific to fraud, dishonesty, breach of trust, or money laundering must never be committed.

g) Waiting period for test retakes

In the event of a failed test, the applicant may retake the exam after a 30-day waiting period for the 2nd and 3rd attempts if needed. If there is a failure on the 3rd attempt, there is a 180-day waiting period, and then the cycle begins anew.

h) Sponsorship requirement

To obtain an MLO license, an applicant also needs to have a sponsor who is an NMLS-licensed entity. The sponsor will have access to the applicant's profile and takes on the responsibility of any actions. Also, the sponsoring entity is not allowed to change information on the MU4 unless the individual provides consent.

i) Definition of "MLO"

An MLO is any person who does both of the following actions:

- Receives a residential mortgage application, and
- Offers or negotiates terms of a residential mortgage loan for financial gain

j) Grounds for denying a license

A license will be denied if the applicant fails to meet one of the requirements. The reasons for denial will be provided and the applicant can reapply if appropriate. Reasons for denying the applicant are failure to comply with the requirements for licensure. This may include:

- Not meeting the minimum pre-licensing requirements
- Failure to pass the SAFE Exam
- History of criminal activity
- Unacceptable creditworthiness
- History of fraud
- Inaccurate application information

An applicant or individual may have their license denied, suspended, revoked, or declined if the applicant or licensee withholds information or makes a material misstatement in an application. No licensee, individual, or person subject to investigation or examination can knowingly withhold any books, records, computer records, or other information. These activities are punishable by law.

k) License maintenance:

i. Renewal period

Renewal periods occur during November and December each year providing MLO's the opportunity to renew their license. The only exception to the requirement to renew during this period is new licensees within the last 6 months of the year. If MLOs fail to renew during this period, they are prohibited from performing any mortgage duties until the renewal is complete and must do so immediately.

ii. Continuing Education requirements

To ensure continued compliance by licensed individuals, the SAFE Act has a continuing education requirement. The requirement is fulfilled by 8 hours of NMLS approved education each year. The training must include the same minimum requirements as the pre-licensure education:

- 3 hours of federal law and regulations
- 3 hours of ethics
- 2 hours of standards on non-traditional mortgage lending

iii. Maintaining an active license

An MLO that does not renew their license in the required time may not participate in activities related to mortgage loans until the renewal is complete.

iv. Retaking 80-3 test if inactive

If a license has been allowed to lapse and has been expired for five years, the results of any tests are no longer valid, and the requirements must be met as if the applicant is beginning from scratch again. Therefore, the same minimum requirements apply.

l) NMLS requirements:

i. Change of employment notifications

Significant changes to status must be updated with the NMLS within 30 days of the occurrence or change. These include:

- Name changes
- Employment termination
- Reportable changes to regulatory actions

Changes in employment must be updated immediately, and no mortgage activities can be performed at the new place of employment until the update is complete. If the fingerprints provided are more than 3 years old, new ones must be submitted.

ii. Required submissions/disclosures

MLO must submit the following to the NMLS system:

- Identifying information such as name, address, social security, etc.
- 10-year employment history
- History of any regulatory actions taken against the employee
- Fingerprints for background check

iii. Required disclosures to NMLS

NMLS must receive the required disclosures to verify the minimum application requirements including:

- Credit history
- Fingerprints for CBC
- All application information
- Employment history

iii. NMLS identifier requirements

The SAFE Act prohibits individuals from participating in the business of mortgage loan origination without obtaining and maintaining:

- For those employed by a covered financial institution, Federal registration as an MLO and a unique identifier
- For all others, a state license, registration, and unique identifier

MLO's are required to display their identifiers to consumers in a practical way. This may be achieved by:

- Directing consumers to a listing of MLO's on the institution's website
- Providing the information prominently in a publicly accessible place
- When requested by consumers

The NMLS identifier must be provided by the licensee in the following situations:

- Before committing to a mortgage transaction
- Upon written or verbal request
- In any initial communication with a consumer

m) Temporary Authority to Originate – Economic Growth, Regulatory Relief, and Consumer Protection Act

Temporary authority may be permitted if the individual is employed by a state-licensed mortgage company and is either registered in NMLS as an MLO continuously during the one-year period preceding the application submission or is licensed as an MLO continuously during the 30-day period preceding the application date. The temporary status enables the following:

- Change of employment of qualified MLOs
- MLOs looking to become licensed in another state,

MLOs are not eligible if any of the following are true:

- Denied MLO license application
- Revoked or suspended license
- Received a cease and desist order
- Convicted of a misdemeanor or felony

The timetable for temporary authority starts at the time an eligible MLO submits a complete license application. It will end upon the earliest of the following:

- Application withdrawal
- State denial
- The granting of the license
- 120 days after the application submission date

4. Compliance:

a) State regulator's authority to examine a licensee's books and records and interview employees

State regulators have the authority to conduct investigations into situations where they have a reason to believe there has been inappropriate conduct. Financial institutions must comply and be willing participants in any investigations, including:

- Providing documents and records
- Comply with auditing
- Adhere to sanctions or penalties

CFPB has the authority to issue a civil investigation and to direct the person in question to produce documents for inspection or copying. The investigations are authorized under the Dodd-Frank Act.

Request for documents and information for the purposes of the examination shall be provided by the entity to be examined

In investigations, financial institutions are held to the requirements of proper record retention and must provide those records upon request. The CFPB during investigations will often require testimony or responses to written questions. The information investigated includes:

- The nature of the conduct
- The applicable law
- Staff involved

Penalties include monetary fines of up to about $5,000 per day for tier 1 penalties, up to about $25,000 per day for tier 2, and up to about $1 million per day for tier 3. In addition, other remedies may be sought such as refunds, paying of damages, or disgorgement of profits.

Compliance of examinations is required by law. All documents and information shall be provided as requested.

Notice of examinations come no later than 60 days prior.

Examinations follow a cycle of four parts:

- Pre-examination and scoping: Review and request available information
- Examination: Onsite and offsite investigations including interviews, observations, and review of policies and procedures.
- Communicate conclusions and required corrective actions
- Monitoring: Includes periodic checks and reviews

Loan documents must be dated and filed appropriately and contain all information required by regulations including appropriate disclosures, any written consent, proper ECOA documentation, etc.

b) Prohibited acts:

i. Paying for real estate agent ads

For advertising to comply with the SAFE Act, the following are minimum requirements to be included in advertisements:

- Full legal name of the mortgage company
- NMLS company ID
- Business phone number
- Business address
- Name of originator
- NMLS ID of originator
- Equal housing opportunity logo

NMLS identifiers shall be included in any advertisements for loan products. This is the case in both print and on-line advertisements.

Prohibited acts for compliance include:

- Withholding of information
- Failure to respond to complaints in the appropriate timeframe
- Failure of proper documentation
- Failure of proper record retention

III. GENERAL MORTGAGE KNOWLEDGE (20%)

A. Qualified and Non-qualified Mortgage Programs

1. Qualified mortgages

Lenders must evaluate a borrower's ability to repay to determine if they can in fact meet the requirements of the loan terms. For a loan to be considered a qualified mortgage, there are minimum requirements that must be met. This ensures a minimum level of credentials for the borrower that provides a reasonable expectation that the loan can be paid back. This includes limiting the debt-to-income ratio of the borrower to 43%. Lenders will receive a level of legal protection for QM compliant mortgage.

A qualified mortgage also has requirements outside of the borrower's qualifications. A qualified loan will not have more risky aspects such as:

- Interest-only payments
- Negative Amortization
- Balloon Payments
- Loan terms longer than 30 years
- Excess points or fees

A qualified loan must meet the cap of the amount of points and fees based on the amount of the loan. It can be determined as follows:

- 3% of the total loan amount for a loan greater than or equal to $100,000
- $3,000 for a loan greater than or equal to $60,000 but less than $100,000
- 5% of the total loan amount for a loan greater than or equal to $20,000 but less than $60,000
- $1,000 for a loan greater than or equal to $12,500 but less than $20,000
- 8% of the total loan amount for a loan less than $12,500

Loans that are exempt from ATR/QM are:

- Open-end credit plans
- Time-share plans
- Reverse mortgage
- Bridge loans
- Short duration construction-to-permanent loans
- Consumer credit transactions secured by vacant land

Qualified Mortgages must have an APR that does not classify it as a higher-priced mortgage. Therefore, if they have an APR that exceeds the APOR by 1.5 percentage points or more for first-lien loans and 3.5 percentage points or more for subordinate-lien loans they are not qualified.

Types of qualified mortgages include:

- General: Loans which fall under the normal requirements of the qualified mortgage. This includes:
    - 43% maximum DTI ratio
    - No risky features
    - Loan term maximum of 30 years
    - Asset verifications
    - Maximum fees and points limit of 3%
    - Fully amortized loan
- Temporary: Loans which meet all of the requirements of the general loans but must be eligible for purchase by Fannie Mae or Freddie Mac. These loans are not necessarily subject to the 43% DTI maximum
- Small Creditor: These are loans provided by small creditors. This is defined as less than $2 billion in assets and originates less than 500 mortgages per year. These QM's have the same requirements of general loans

2. Conventional/conforming

a) Includes Fannie Mae and Freddie Mac

Fannie Mae and Freddie Mac are government entities that purchase most of the home loans in the US and provide liquidity to lenders as needed. This allows lenders to be able to have the assets necessary to provide a larger and wide-ranging number of loans. This is done by Fannie Mae and Freddie Mac packaging loans into attractive mortgage-backed securities in which payment is more dependable. This helps to stabilize the market and lower interest rates based on the reduced risk. The sister company, Ginnie Mae, is the entity responsible for payments of mortgage bonds and does not fall under Fannie Mae and Freddie Mac's responsibilities.

For conventional loans, seller concessions are limited depending on the amount of the down payment and whether the residence is primary or an investment property:

- Primary residence or second home:
    - Less than 10% down: 3% Maximum
    - 10%-25% down: 6% Maximum
    - 25% or more: 9% Maximum

- Investment property:
    - 2% Maximum regardless of down payment

Risk-based fees are applied to loans called Loan-Level Pricing Adjustments (LLPA). They vary based on loan-to-value (LTV), credit score, occupancy type, and the number of units in a home. Borrowers often pay LLPAs in the form of higher mortgage rates.

The loan-level pricing adjustment is based on identifying risk characteristics which indicate an increased risk on a loan. LLPAs are cumulative so if a loan includes 3 LLPA's, all three are applied.

Loan traits which affect your loan-level pricing adjustment include:

- Investment property
- Condo with less than 25% equity
- Multi-unit home
- A cash-out refinance

LLPA's do not apply to FHA, VA, or USDA loans.

Automated Underwriting Systems provide computer-generated underwriting decisions on loans based on input. While they can be flexible for decisions on a number of loans, they are best for conventional or typical loans with standard procedures or amortization. There are a number of different options for automated underwriting systems such as Fannie Mae uses Desktop Underwriter while Freddie Mac uses Loan Prospector.

Non-owner occupied properties are a classification for one to four-unit investment properties. They are evaluated differently since the property is not the owner's primary residence and there is projected income from the property itself. Some of the differences include:

- Higher interest rates and fees due to increased risks
- Higher down payment minimums
- Higher required reserve funds
- Not available for government-backed loans
- Projected cash flow from rental included in the application assessment

Conventional loans often require higher minimum down payment amounts than government-backed loans such as FHA which requires 3.5% or VA which can be as low as 0%. While low down payment loans exist, lenders will not often accept less than 5% down and anything less than 20% will require Private Mortgage Insurance (PMI). The cost of the PMI is determined based on the down payment and other factors such as credit score.

Prepayment penalties are a choice for a lender to impose on a borrower. For prepayment penalties to be allowed, all of the following must be true:

- The APR must remain constant
- The loan is qualified
- The loan is not a higher-priced loan

Additionally, there are certain restrictions on penalties.

- A prepayment penalty is capped at 2% for the first two years and 1% thereafter.
- A prepayment penalty can only exist for the first 3 years
- The lender must offer a non-prepayment penalty loan option

3. Government

a) Includes FHA, VA, USDA

FHA mortgage is one that is insured by the Federal Housing Administration (FHA) and provided by an FHA approved lender.

FHA loans are government-backed loans. Therefore, an FHA loan has a low minimum down payment of 3.5%, but the credit score of the individual must be at least 580. If the credit score falls between 500 and 580 the minimum down payment increases to 10%. FHA has maximum debt ratios which are 31% on the front end and 43% on the back end. The loans actually come from an FHA approved lender and not FHA itself. The backing of the loan comes from the required upfront mortgage insurance premium cost that is included as a part of the closing costs. This does not relieve the borrower of the annual PMI requirement. In addition to traditional mortgages, FHA also offers the following:

- Home equity conversion loans
- 203k home improvement loans
- Energy-efficient mortgage program
- Graduated payment loans

The Federal Housing Authority (FHA) is a Government Agency which protects lenders from mortgage default.

The US Department of Agriculture (USDA) provides loans for individuals seeking property in a rural or suburban area. The loans are issued through the Rural Development Guaranteed Housing Loan Program. Similarly, to FHA loans, these loans are backed by the USDA. To be eligible the purchase must be for an owner-occupied primary residence and must also meet the following requirements:

- US Citizenship
- Typically, a maximum 29% front end and 41% back-end debt ratio
- Qualifying, sustainable income
- Acceptable credit history

Some of the main benefits of USDA loans are lower interest rates and the ability to put 0% down on the mortgage.

VA loans are available for veterans to receive more beneficial loans. The loans are issued by private lenders but backed by the US Department of Veteran affairs. Some of the benefits of the VA loans include:

- 0% down payment
- No PMI
- Lower interest rates
- Easier to qualify

While mortgage insurance serves a purpose for the protection of lenders, it must not be a hindrance to the borrower. Certain limits are placed on PMI so that it does not become unnecessarily excessive.

PMI shall not be required for LTV's of 80% or less. In addition, the Homeowners Protection Act mandates that lenders disclose the necessary information to borrowers regarding the PMI process and scenarios. PMI also must automatically stop for borrowers who reach a specified amount of equity in the loan.

The determination of the interest rate for FHA mortgages is determined by a number of factors similar to conventional loans including:

- Credit score
- Amount of loan
- Down payment
- Type of rate
- Discount points

Guarantors are government agencies that guarantee repayment of mortgages. This is often done by the use of mortgage insurance. The largest entities include:

- Federal Housing Authority (FHA)
- Department of Veteran's Affairs (VA)
- Rural Housing Service (RHS)
- Office of Public Land and Indian Housing
- Government National Mortgage Association (GNMA)

VA entitlement is a benefit to veterans seeking a first-time mortgage. It refers to the amount of money that is guaranteed to lenders in the event of default. While VA loans can require 0% down, there is a limit based on the entitlement. There are two scenarios to determine the amount:

- $36,000 for loans less than $144,000
- 25% of loans greater than $144,000

A Certificate of Eligibility (COE) verifies to the lender that the applicant is eligible for a VA loan. To obtain the certificate, the borrower must provide evidence of service depending on their status:

- For Veterans/Current or former National Guard/Reserve members who have been activated for Federal active service
    - DD Form 214
- Active Duty Servicemember
    - A current statement of service
- Current National Guard or Reserve member not Federal active service
    - Statement of Service

Funds must be verified and documented prior to closing to be used for closing costs or down payments. Often lenders will require funds to be seasoned meaning they have been in the account for a certain period of time often at least two months or more. Funds from unreliable or unacceptable potential sources shall not be used such as a pay advance. Acceptable source of funds may include:

- Savings and checking accounts
- The borrower's earnest money deposit
- Acceptable gift funds
- Savings bonds
- Investment/retirement accounts (401k, IRA, Keogh)

- Stocks and bonds
- Proceeds from the sale of another home or personal property
- Proceeds from the sale of other personal property
- Income/equity generated from a rental property
- Sweat equity

The FHA establishes minimum property standards that may cause properties acceptable under conventional loans, to not be eligible for FHA financing. The standard is established to protect both the lender and the borrower from entering into an agreement with a sub-standard property which may require extensive repairs or limit the ability of a resale.

The minimum standards can be divided into three categories:

- Safety: Any aspects of the property which may be considered a risk to the safety of the occupant or any visiting individuals must be addressed. This may include certain areas of the home which are not up to code such as railing heights or tripping hazards
- Security: The home should adequately protect the occupant and possessions inside
- Soundness: The property may not have aspects that may compromise the structural integrity of the home. This may include rotting of structural supports or excessive foundation cracking

FHA will assess the severity of the defect and does not require the repair of anything determined to be minor or cosmetic

FHA sets limits on the amount that can be borrowed. It is dependent on the geographical area in which the loan is taken and the median sale price in that area. However, it can never be higher than the ceiling or lower than the floor in any area. Single-family forward loan limits are 115% of median house prices, subject to the floor and ceiling on the limits. Any areas where the loan limit exceeds this floor is considered a high-cost area, and FHA is required to set its maximum loan limit ceiling for high-cost areas at 150% of the national conforming limit.

A funding fee of 2.15% for VA loans is required by all but certain exempt veterans. A down payment of 5 percent or more will change it to 1.5%. A 10% payment further reduced it to 1.25%.

All Reserve or National Guard must pay 2.40%. A down payment of 5 percent or more will reduce the fee to 1.75%, and a 10 percent down payment will reduce it to 1.5%.

The following are exemptions to paying the funding fee:

- Those who get VA compensation for service-connected disabilities.

- Veterans who would be entitled to receive compensation for service-connected disabilities if they did not receive retirement pay.
- Surviving spouses of veterans who died in service or from service-connected disabilities

The funding fee is eligible to be financed as a part of the loan.

FHA loans will require an upfront mortgage insurance premium (UFMIP). This is required to be able to provide the borrower with a reduced down payment amount to offset the risk the lender is taking with the reduced equity. This is a one-time payment as a part of the closing costs. This does not replace the need for the monthly mortgage insurance. The UFMIP will typically be about 1.75% of the total loan amount.

VA residual income is a measure of the amount of income left over monthly after the mortgage and expenses. It is a more realistic look at an applicant's ability to afford a mortgage payment. The minimum is then a function of the size of the family, the geographical location, and whether or not the loan is above or below $80,000.

For a VA loan, in addition to the normally required information, the following is also required

- Copy of DD214 if separated from the military
- Completed Request for Certificate of Eligibility (COE)
- Statement of service from a commanding officer if active duty
- Certificate of Eligibility

PMI is a function of the down payment provided for a loan and the creditworthiness of an applicant. It typically will vary from 0.5% to 2.5% annually of the loan amount.

The minimum down payment for an FHA loan is as low as 3.5%. However, this is based on credit score as this is only for those at 580 or greater. A credit score of 500 to 580 may still achieve a loan, but the minimum raises to 10% down.

4. Conventional/nonconforming

A non-conforming loan does not meet the requirements for a mortgage by the government entities Fannie Mae and Freddie Mac. This will result in the lender not being able to sell the loan to the government as often happens. Some guidelines that the Government Sponsored Entities (GSE) require include among others:

- Maximum loan amount
- Suitable properties
- Down payment minimums

- Creditworthiness

These loans are seen as riskier to the lenders and will often require a higher interest rate to the borrower.

Payment shock is a concern that lenders may have when an individual has a dramatic increase in monthly obligations. The threshold can be set by a certain percentage or a function of the debt-to-income ratio.

a) Jumbo, Alt-A

A jumbo loan exceeds the limits set by the Federal Housing Finance Administration (FHFA) and its main function is to finance luxury homes or those in highly competitive markets. Due to the exceeding of limits, they are riskier and not eligible to be bought or guaranteed by Fannie Mae and Freddie Mac.

Jumbo loans due to being riskier in nature will have more strict requirements than conforming. This includes higher down payments, more documentation, a higher credit score and some other factors. A limit for the debt-to-income ratio may be as low as 30% but at times can be much higher such as 45%.

b) Subprime mortgage

Subprime mortgages are those who belong to less qualified borrowers. The characteristics of these borrowers are discussed below

Subprime borrowers are less qualified than others. Their characteristics may include:

- Low FICO score (less than 660)
- History of delinquent payments such as two or more of greater than 30 days in the last 12 months or one of 60 days or more.
- A foreclosure
- A bankruptcy
- A high debt-to-income ratio (typically 50% or higher)

These borrowers are less desirable since the loans are less likely to be sold as mortgage-backed securities to the government entities and are at a higher risk of default.

c) Guidance on nontraditional mortgage product risk

Nontraditional mortgages cover a wide range of mortgage types. They refer to those that do not fit common mortgage characteristics, such as standard amortization characteristics or installment payments. They are used in unique situations or for less qualified and subprime borrowers. Some types of nontraditional mortgages include:

- Balloon loans
- Interest-only payment loans
- Payment option adjustable-rate mortgages
- Negative amortization loan

Since nontraditional mortgages have unique circumstances, there is a reasonable amount of increased risk that will be associated with them. The borrower is often able to receive lower monthly payments or advantages in the short term, but there is a long-term risk that the lender must account for. This often results in increased interest rates or increased payments as the loan progresses throughout the term. The borrower is at risk if circumstances change from the original intention and may be stuck with an undesirable loan later on.

The determination of the borrower's ability-to-repay becomes more complicated in nontraditional loans. The underwriter must consider the fluctuations of the loan throughout the life and the borrower's situation at these times. A borrower may be able to qualify for initial lower payments, but less so once introductory rates or payments expire. This will be taken into consideration for approval.

Nontraditional mortgages can be considered by borrowers in certain situations where the terms are determined to be advantageous. The most common situations are those where the borrower has no intention of staying in a property for the long term. If a residence will be temporary, a lower monthly payment or a period of a lower interest rate may be appropriate. For example, someone who has a job for only a time of 4 years and will then sell may be able to use a 5/1 ARM to take advantage of the lower rate and then sell before reaching the adjustable portion of the mortgage. Another common situation is developers looking to resell the property over a short period of time.

The risk associated with changing market or personal conditions should be considered for individuals seeking nontraditional loans. A property's value can decrease significantly and unexpectedly over a short period of time.

Consumers must be clearly shown and explained the terms of the loan that is being presented. The consumer can sometimes have a lack of understanding of the fluctuations of a loan over its life. Being shortsighted is also a common pitfall as they can be blinded by the desirability of short-term payments or rates. It is required by law that no false advertising or representation be made to the consumer so that they have a full understanding of the financial agreement.

d) Non-qualified mortgage

Non-qualified loans are those which do not fit the requirements of qualified loans. They are not necessarily high-risk loans , and there are certain circumstances where they are appropriate. They may be for self-employed borrowers with a short income history, often less than 2 years. While the requirements are different from qualified mortgages, a minimum credit score is still required. Non-QM's can also be for loans greater than 30 years or a high DTI provided there is a demonstration that it can be overcome with substantial reserves.

As stated before, non-qualified mortgages are those that simply do not fit the QM requirements. Therefore, these may include those loans which do not fit the ability-to-repay rule but are still approved by the lender. Some examples include:

- Loans with terms longer than 30 years.
- Interest-only payment loans
- Balloon loans
- Negative amortization loans

B. Mortgage Loan Products

1. Fixed-rate mortgages

Fixed-rate mortgages include an interest rate that will not change over the full life of the loan. Because of this, there is a constant payment for the principal and interest for the full amortization schedule of the loan. The total home payment can change due to variances in the property taxes, insurance, or PMI.

When comparing fixed rates for loans, a borrower should ensure they are looking at the total cost of borrowing and not just the number. Often lower rates may not be the best option when considering other associated fees that will make the APR increase.

A fixed-rate mortgage by its nature will not change by the principal and interest payment alone. The changes to the monthly payment will be a result of only a change in the other portions of the payment, including taxes or hazard insurance.

Adding additional payments to a mortgage beyond the minimum requirements will reduce the principal balance and the life of the loan. For a fixed-rate mortgage, this does not affect the monthly payments despite the reduction in interest over the life of the loan. The paydown can work to eliminate PMI if it is existing on the loan which will reduce the monthly obligations.

A fixed-rate mortgage monthly payment will most often consist of the principal, interest, PMI (if applicable), and escrow. Escrow will include payments for the property taxes and insurance required to ensure they will be paid on time with sufficient funds. While a fixed-rate mortgage will not vary based on the principal and interest rate, the escrow can be a source of change as taxes and insurance will often change yearly.

2. Adjustable-rate mortgages (ARMs)

Adjustable-rate mortgages are those which will vary throughout the life of the loan. It often includes a period of time with a fixed rate and then switches to an adjustable one which is evaluated in predefined intervals. They are denoted by two numbers, the first being the fixed period and the second being the timeframe in which the rate is adjusted. For example, a 5/1 ARM is fixed for the first 5 years and then is adjusted once every year thereafter. The adjusted rate is a combination of the margin and the index. The margin for an ARM most likely will remain the same over time, but the index is subject to change.

When choosing an adjustable-rate mortgage, the borrower can decide how to proceed with payments based on the individual situation. The following are typical ARM payment options:

- A fully amortizing payment with a 30- or 40-year lifespan
- A fully amortizing payment with a 15-year lifespan
- A loan which includes interest-only payments
- A minimum payment loan

The margin is the fixed portion of the fully indexed rate. It will not vary throughout the life of the loan. Margins are more similar to typical fixed rates as they are determined during the application process and are a function of the borrower's creditworthiness. Therefore, a low credit score will yield a high margin and vice versa.

The index is the portion of an adjustable-rate that varies throughout the life of the loan and is determined at each evaluation period. The index is often referred to as a benchmark interest rate since it is reliant on a specific index determined by the lender before closing. Some common indexes which can be used are:

- Maturity yield on one-year Treasury Bills
- 11th District cost of funds index

- London Interbank Offered rate

The fully indexed rate is the addition of the fixed margin rate and the variable index rate as determined by the agreed-upon index. This is the rate used to determine the monthly payment during a period of the loan:

$$Fully\ Indexed\ Rate = Margin + Index$$

Adjustable-rate mortgages are denoted by the time period in which the rate is fixed and then the frequency over which the rate is evaluated and adjusted. The types of ARM's include:

- Hybrid: Includes a fixed-rate period and then a rate that changes based on a defined time period. This may include 5/1, 3/1, 15/15 and so on.
- Interest-only: Includes a fixed rate interest-only period and then adjustable after.
- Payment option: This allows the borrower to choose between options of payment. The options include interest-only payment, a fully amortized payment, or a lesser minimum payment of interest only. The borrower option is only for a set period and then the loan reverts to a more traditional situation.

In addition to the escrow related payment changes as described in the fixed-rate section, adjustable rates are also subject to the change in payment due to the change in the interest rate. Any time the rate changes, the monthly payment will be adjusted accordingly. This is determined by the calculation of the fully indexed rate, and then this rate is applied to the principal balance to determine the new payment amount.

An adjustable-rate loan has a rate that may fluctuate throughout the life or a portion of the loan term. The rate for the adjustable period is determined by the fully indexed rate which is the margin plus the index. ARM's have caps that the rate cannot exceed regardless of the index and margin. The lifetime cap limits the increase over the life of the loan and the periodic cap limits the increase from one period to the next.

Fully indexed rates are calculated by adding the margin and index together but while adhering to the determined cap limits. The rate must never exceed the lifetime cap, and the change cannot exceed the periodic cap.

The change date is the contractual date at which the rate will be adjusted. This will increase or decrease the adjustable-rate until the next adjustment date. The monthly payment will be adjusted according to the change in the fully indexed rate.

Notice is required for the initial rate change:

The first time the interest rate adjusts, a notice must be at least 210 days, but not more than 240 days, before the first payment at the new adjusted level is due.

Notice is required for each subsequent rate change:

Each time the interest rate subsequently adjusts and results in a change to the payment amount, a notice must be sent at least 60 days, but no more than 120 days, before the first payment at the adjusted level is due.

In general interest rates are determined as a combination of the following factors:

- Credit score
- Home location
- Property cost
- Down payment
- Loan term
- Loan type

Adjustable rates are subject to the indexes as mentioned.

When calculating the monthly payment for an ARM, the period in which the rate is fixed is calculated in the same fashion as a fixed-rate mortgage which includes the principal and interest, taxes, insurance and PMI. For the period where there is an ARM, the calculation must additionally include the adjustable-rate terms, rate caps, expected rate changes, and time in between adjustments. While the payment changes, the rate will still fully amortize over the life of the loan.

If the annual percentage rate on a loan may increase after consummation, and the term of the loan exceeds one year, TILA requires additional disclosures to be provided:

- A loan program disclosure for each variable-rate program in any instance in which the applicant shows intent to purchase.
- The Consumer Handbook on Adjustable Rate Mortgages published by the Federal Home Loan Bank Board. This also may be replaced by an acceptable substitute.

TILA requires subsequent disclosure to consumers each time an interest rate adjustment takes place.

The CHARM handbook is an additional disclosure required for consumers of adjustable-rate mortgages. It is designed to help consumers understand more complex mortgage products. It outlines what ARMs are and provides examples of payments. Other topics include payment shock, discount points, and rate caps.

3. Purchase money second mortgages

A Purchase money second mortgage is a subordinate loan for a portion of the purchase price of a home. Loans which include a second mortgage are denoted by the percentages made up by each aspect of the loan in the format: First Mortgage-Second Mortgage-Down Payment. This is used typically in lieu of a down payment for a home purchase. It is a second, separate loan that can enable a borrower to finance up to 100% of the home.

4. Balloon mortgages

Balloon loans include a lump sum payment portion of the principal balance instead of fully amortizing with payments over the life of the loan. Consumers will pay a portion of the loan or an interest-only period which has lower payments. Then at the end, there is a remaining balance that must be paid. Balloon loans are considered high-risk options.

Balloon mortgages are often structured as a two-step process. The first includes lower payments for a specific amount of time on a portion of the principal balance. The second phase then incorporates the remaining amount of the principal into a new loan with higher payments. The outstanding balance may also be refinanced or paid in full at the end of the term in some cases.

Regulation Z requires lenders to thoroughly investigate the borrower's ability to repay for balloon loans. Lenders shall not evaluate the borrower solely based on the initial payment amounts. They must look at the borrower's ability to repay at least in some fashion after the end of the initial terms including other options such as refinancing. In no way shall the borrower be approved for being put into a position where they cannot reasonably handle the monthly obligations at any point during the loan.

The characteristics of a balloon loan are advantages for scenarios where the borrower will benefit from initial lower payments. The disadvantage comes later when the remaining portion of the balance is active, and the payments will increase significantly. This can be useful for those who have a short-term intention of staying in the home or will have a significant jump in income at a later date in the loan. There is a significant risk with balloon loans if there is a plan to sell the home before the balloon phase becomes active. Changing housing markets can cause unforeseen issues while being obligated to now pay a higher monthly payment for a borrower.

5. Reverse mortgages

A reverse mortgage provides payment from a lender to a borrower that taps into the existing equity of a home. The equity is reduced as the payments are made. The lender is not buying the home however and the borrower is indeed still responsible for the increase in debt that results from the payments. This is often settled by the selling of the home at the completion of the loan.

The qualification for a reverse mortgage depends on a number of factors including age and interest rates. However, an applicant does not need 100% equity to be considered for a reverse mortgage. The requirement is you must be able to pay off your existing mortgage with the amount received.

Interest on a HECM is calculated based on the agreed terms of the loan. It could be a fixed amount based on a fixed rate every month. It also can be variable which may include a one-time payment or a calculated monthly payment until the loan recipient experiences an action that would necessitate the loan being repaid.

There are fees associated with closing on a reverse mortgage. These include:

- Origination fee: Upfront charge for the lender to originate the loan
- Mortgage insurance cost: HUD requires all reverse mortgages to have mortgage insurance. This ensures payments will continue regardless of the financial institution's situation. There is an upfront and monthly cost
- Third-party closing costs: Any additional service needed such as inspections or appraisals.

Conversion mortgages or reverse mortgages have a minimum age requirement of 62 years old.

The title insurance may not be less than the greater of:

- Fair market value of the property
- Maximum amount of principal as stated in the mortgage

The amount of permissible equity which can be withdrawn is determined by the principal limit factor. This is a percentage of the total amount of property value that can be taken out. It is common to be up to 0.60 and sometimes lower. There is an absolute maximum regardless of the amount of equity that may vary from state to state.

Situations in which the full balance may become due include:

- Death of the borrower
- No longer using the property as a primary residence
- Failure to pay property taxes or insurance

- Failure to maintain the property in an acceptable state or repair

Advertisements for reverse mortgages must not be deceptive and shall be truthful in the available products. Some of the key points to follow includes:

- Prohibition of deceptive or misleading product descriptions
    - Inform borrowers of all available features
    - Explain features in plain language
- Include specific disclaimers for scenarios where HUD or FHA did not approve the material
- Comply with Federal requirements regarding the use of HUD and FHA logos
- Proper record retention

Regulation Z has specific requirements for disclosures that lenders must provide to the borrower. These include:

- Itemized list of pertinent information including
    - Minimum age requirement
    - Terms
    - Charges
    - Property values
- Annual loan cost rates and explanation
- Costs to obtain the loan
- Loan estimate must be provided

6. Home equity line of credit (HELOC)

Open-end credit is any type of loan where you can make repeated withdrawals and repayments. Examples include credit cards, home equity loans, and personal lines of credit.

The Home Equity Line of Credit (HELOC) is a way for a borrower to tap into the equity of an existing home loan for other purposes. HELOC's and home equity loans are, but there are some differences. One of which is that the home equity loan typically will have a fixed rate while the HELOC will be an adjustable-rate with interest calculated per diem. The line of credit can be accessed up to the maximum amount agreed upon by the borrower and lender. The borrower can use as much or as little as they wish. HELOCs often have a draw period in which there are interest-only payments and then a repayment period where the payment includes both interest and principal.

7. Construction mortgages

There are two types of loans for construction: construction-to-permanent loans and stand-alone construction loans. The construction-to-permanent is a single loan comprised of two parts. Therefore, there is only one closing, and terms can be set on the mortgage after construction such as a maximum rate. The payments made during construction are interest only.

A construction only loan is actually two separate loans: one solely for the construction of the home and then a mortgage. Because of this the fees for the loans are separate and require two sets

The disclosures for construction loans shall be clearly designated as needed. This includes the creditor disclosing the loan being for "construction."

The required payments for the loan depend on the type:

Construction-to-permanent loan: This includes a single loan with two phases. The first includes interest-only payments with variable rates. Once construction is complete, the required payments convert to a typical mortgage.

Stand-alone construction loans: Payments are separated into two separate loans that have their own terms, rates, and requirements.

Construction-to-permanent loans include a construction phase and a post-construction phase. The loans are combined into one loan. During the construction phase, the borrower pays only interest on the outstanding principal. During this time the rate is often variable, and the payment will fluctuate according to the variability. Once construction is complete, the loan is converted into a permanent mortgage. This may include variable terms and a fixed or variable rate mortgage. Construction loans often require a large down payment and a significant amount of reserve funds to account for uncertainty during construction. There must be an accounting for construction contingency in which the construction estimate is found to not be sufficient which is very common.

8. Interest-only mortgages

Interest-only mortgages as the name suggests, includes payments that consist only of paying interest. This means that there is no pay down of the principal balance as the loan progresses. These mortgages will have a set period of interest only and then begin a phase of increased payments that include a portion for the paying down the principal.

Interest-only payments do not pay down the principal balance. The payment is most often based on a fixed rate throughout the life of the loan. The payment will increase substantially once the principal amortization period is initiated. At this point, the borrower may refinance or pay off the loan. A typical interest-only period is 10 years with a full length of a loan of 30 years.

C. Terms Used in the Mortgage Industry

1. Loan terms: subordinate loans, escrow accounts, lien, tolerances, rate lock agreement, table funding

A lien is a financial stake in an asset. Junior liens are loans that use an existing asset as collateral that already has an existing loan. For mortgages, this is often a home equity loan with a first mortgage that has yet to be fully paid off. There is a hierarchy of liens that must be paid off in order of seniority. The original mortgage must be paid off first and then any junior liens thereafter in order of the oldest being paid off first.

Subordinate loans, sometimes referred to as subordinated debts, are similar to the concept of junior liens. A subordinate loan ranks below the primary loan and will not be paid off in the event of default until the loans higher in ranking are paid first. Due to this, there is a significant amount of more risk if a loan is subordinate and terms may be unfavorable.

Escrow accounts are where assets are held by a third party until payment is required or obligations are fulfilled. For mortgage purposes, this is very common for a borrower to provide taxes and insurance into an escrow account which is held by the lender. This ensures that payment will be made in the appropriate amount and on time, therefore, reducing the risk taken on by the lender. Escrow accounts are required in FHA loans and conventional loans with an LTV of greater than 80%. In other situations, the borrower can request to waive the requirement for escrow but may be subject to fees.

Table funding is the arrangement of funds being made available concurrently with the time of the loan documents being signed.

Rate lock agreements occur between a lender and a potential borrower to lock in a specific interest rate to avoid the fluctuations of the market. This is often associated with a rate lock fee which increases as the rate lock time period increases. Typically rate lock periods are 10, 30, 45, or 60 days. An extension may be requested at the time of expiration but may incur an additional fee.

TILA-RESPA Integrated Disclosure Rule has 3 types of tolerance thresholds. This is to ensure a good faith standard of estimates and to allow the borrower to prepare for the required fees. The three types are:

- Zero tolerance: As the name implies, there may be no increase from estimate to closing disclosure
- 10% cumulative tolerance: The cumulative change in all fees must not be more than 10%
- No or unlimited tolerance: Any change is acceptable

2. Disclosure terms: yield spread premiums, federal mortgage loans, servicing transfers, lender credits

A yield spread premium is a form of compensation to the broker. It is based on selling an interest rate to a borrower that is higher than the lender's par rate based on the borrower's qualifications. They are also known as negative points. These are the opposite of buying points for a lower interest rate as the rate increases.

Federal mortgage loans are those which are federally backed by the Federal Housing Authority (FHA).

A servicing transfer is the handing over of management of a loan to a new servicing company. This does not have any effect on the borrower as payment will be collected in the same manner.

Lender credits are funds provided by the lender to help cover closing costs. These costs can be rolled into the mortgage loan so that the borrower does not have to have the funds upfront. This comes at an overall cost however as they are often associated with an increase in the mortgage rate.

3. Financial terms: discount points, 2-1 buy-down, loan-to-value (LTV) ratio, accrued interest, finance charges, daily simple interest

Discount points allow the borrower an option to save money on interest over the life of the loan if they choose. The points are beneficial if the borrower will maintain the loan for a period of time that will exceed the breakeven point. This is when the savings from interest exceed the initial upfront cost of the points. Each point typically is worth 1% of the loan and lowers the interest rate by 0.25%.

2-1 buydown is a mortgage option that allows the borrower to reduce the interest rate on a loan for a period of time during the initial years of the loan. The rate will decrease in a stepped fashion by reducing once for a certain period of time and then again for another specified amount of time before reaching the full rate and payment amount. This allows the borrower to initially have a lower interest payment during the early years of the loan if the situation is needed.

For example, a rate of 5.0% may have a 2-1 buydown which includes a 2% reduction for the first year and then a 1% reduction for the second year.

Accrued interest is the amount of interest that has accumulated over a period of time since the inception of the loan or since the previous payment. For mortgages, this will be the amount of interest that has accrued each month in between payments. Accrued interest is determined based on the period in which the interest is calculated. For example, if daily interest is required, it will be calculated every day, whereas monthly will be calculated once per month.

Loan to value ratio is simply the amount financed divided by the value of the home as determined either by the sale price for a purchase transaction or the appraised value for a refinance:

$$LTV = \frac{Amount\ of\ Loan}{Value\ of\ Property}$$

Settlement is the finalizing of the loan. It is typically completed involving a meeting of the buyer, seller, and lender where the property and funds are officially and legally exchanged. This is also referred to as closing.

The finance charge is defined as the total amount of interest and loan charges that the borrower will pay over the entire life of the loan. These are determined based on an assumption that the loan will be repaid in full as scheduled. Loan charges include:

- Discount points
- Mortgage insurance
- Lender charges
- Origination fees

Origination fees are often a percentage of the purchase price, typically 1%. However, there are alternatives and there are instances where it is waived in return for a higher interest rate in which case the fee is paid by means of the yield spread premium.

Debt to income (DTI) ratio is a comparison of a borrower's income to monthly financial obligations:

$$DTI = \frac{(Mortgage + Debt\ Payments)}{Monthly\ Income}$$

The housing ratio also known as the front-end ratio is the housing payment divided by the monthly income:

$$Front\ End\ DTI = \frac{(Mortgage)}{Monthly\ Income}$$

Daily simple interest calculates interest on a daily basis as opposed to monthly like a traditional loan. To calculate, divide the annual rate by 365 days and multiply by the outstanding balance and then multiply by the number of days in the period:

$$Interest = \left(\frac{Annual\ Rate\ as\ a\ decimal}{365}\right)(Loan\ amount)(Number\ of\ days\ in\ period)$$

4. General terms: subordination, conveyance, primary/secondary market, third-party providers, assumable loan, APR

When there are multiple loans involved in a property, there is an agreement of which loan has priority and which are considered junior. A subordination agreement determines the official hierarchy of the loans in the event of default.

Conveyance transfers the legal title of a property between the seller and the buyer. There are four different types of conveyance when real estate is concerned:

- Fee tail: Transfers the interest in the property but restricts any further sale
- Fee simple: Transfers absolute ownership
- Life estate: Transfers ownership for the duration of an individual's life
- Defeasible estate: Transfer of a property with some conditions

A cash out refinance is the same as a normal refinance except the borrower taps into the existing equity and receives a lump sum of a specified amount above the existing principal balance.

Prepaids are payments that are required to be provided before they are due to the appropriate entity. Generally, for mortgages, this refers to the funding of escrow accounts, including property taxes, hazard insurance, and PMI. Lenders will often require that the escrow account includes a minimum amount of reserves to ensure there are sufficient funds in the account. The prepaids will include this buffer along with the required amount that will be needed at the time the bill is due.

Underwriting is the evaluation of a borrower to determine their suitability for a loan. They will evaluate the applicant for their ability-to-repay and determine if the lender shall proceed with issuing the loan.

The primary mortgage market is the name for the transactions involving the origination and execution of mortgage loans. These loans are then packaged and sold in the secondary mortgage market.

The secondary mortgage market is where mortgages are bought and sold as securities. An aggregator is an entity that purchases mortgages from financial institutions and then securitizes them into mortgage-backed securities (MBS).

Third-party providers are authorized service providers that are involved in a banking transaction but exist outside of the relationship between a borrower and a bank.

An assumable loan allows a borrower to take on an existing loan, including all aspects of that loan such as the term and interest rate.

The annual percentage rate (APR) is the total cost to the borrower for borrowing the principal. This includes the interest rate and any other costs associated with the loan. These include:

- Points
- Broker fees
- Closing costs

Not all fees are included in the calculation of the APR such as appraisal, credit reporting, or inspection fees.

APOR is a survey-based rate resulting from the average rates for prime mortgages. The APOR can be provided for a range of loan terms from 1 to 50 years. The rate is provided by the Federal Financial Institutions Examination Council (FFIEC) and is available daily. The APOR is used in the classifying loans of high-cost or high-priced.

Higher priced mortgages are those which have an Annual Percentage Rate (APR) which is higher than a benchmark rate called the Average Prime Offer Rate (APOR). Higher priced mortgages are deemed to be more difficult to be paid back and are therefore subject to additional requirements from lenders. Regulation Z section 1026.35 provides the requirements for higher-priced mortgage loans.

The determination of a higher-priced mortgage is by the loan type:

- First-lien mortgage: If APR is 1.5 percentage points higher than APOR
- Jumbo loan: If APR is 2.5 percentage points higher than APOR
- Subordinate-lien mortgage: If APR is 3.5 percentage points higher than APOR

Higher priced mortgages are subject to the following additional requirements:

- Required escrow accounts
- Certified appraisals must be performed

A high-cost loan, not to be confused with a higher-priced loan, has characteristics which are non-traditional. The aspects which meet the criteria for a high-cost loan are:

- APR exceeds the APOR by more than 6.5%
- Points and fees exceed 5% of the loan
- The loan has a prepayment penalty either beyond 36 months of the initiation of the loan or exceeds 2% of the amount prepaid

IV. MORTGAGE LOAN ORIGINATION ACTIVITIES (27%)

A. Loan Inquiry and Application Process Requirements

1. Loan inquiry process – includes required disclosures

Form 1003 is the Uniform Residential Loan Application. The form was developed by Fannie Mae and Freddie Mac and it is the industry standard form for the process of a loan application. In general, the form is filled out twice. Once at the time of initial application and then at closing. The form includes all of the following:

- Income
- Assets
- Liabilities
- 2-year employment history

Lenders and mortgage brokers are required to provide a borrower with the following after a loan application:

- Special Information Booklet for settlement services
- Loan Estimate
- Mortgage Servicing Disclosure Statement

Mortgage application information needs to be provided by law accurately to the reasonable knowledge of the applicant. The required information includes:

- Name
- Social Security
- Property address included in the transaction
- Income
- Loan amount
- Employment history
- Resident history
- Assets
- Debts
- Credit history including bankruptcy or foreclosures

Lenders and mortgage brokers are required to provide a borrower with the following after a loan application:

- Special Information Booklet for settlement services
- Loan Estimate
- Mortgage Servicing Disclosure Statement

2. Borrower application:

a) Accepting applications

For an application to be received and complete, it must include at a minimum:

- Consumer name
- Consumer income
- Social Security number
- Property address
- Estimate of the value of the property
- Loan amount sought

b) Offering/negotiating terms

Offering and negotiating the terms of a loan for an MLO includes:

- Presenting a loan offer to a consumer for acceptance which may include:
  - Further verification of information
  - The offer having conditional statements
  - Work by other individuals to complete the loan process
- Responding to the consumer if they are requesting different terms such as a lower rate or less points on the loan
- Presenting to the consumer a revised loan offer

c) Managing information

Mortgage Loan Originators are in charge of ensuring the applications are filled out properly and all necessary information is provided. Tasks for the MLO include:

- Ensuring all documents are provided
- Ensure minimum information is required
- Ensure appropriate disclosures are provided
- Analyze information for discrepancies and inconsistencies
- Verify the information is correct and accurate

d) Permissible questions

Lenders are able to pursue all information that can be considered relevant to evaluating the applicant's ability to repay. This includes income, credit history, assets, liabilities, and employment. Additionally, the lender may ask ethnicity to avoid discrimination and legal history.

Lenders may not ask about family planning or health issues and how they may relate to the applicant's financial situation.

e) Gift donors

A donor as per Fannie Mae requirements, must be a relative by blood, marriage, adoption, or legal guardian. They also shall not be any other interested party to the transaction.

If a borrower is to use a gift to cover costs on a mortgage, there are situations in which there must be a contribution from the borrower's own funds. For a conventional loan with 20% down, the gift is allowed to cover all of the funds. For less than 20% there are restrictions on how much of the gift can cover costs and it varies by loan type. For FHA and VA loans the gift may cover all costs regardless of down payment amount as long as the credit score is 620 or greater. If the credit score is less, the borrower is responsible for 3.5% of the down payment.

3. Verification:

a) Authorization forms

The Certification and Authorization form is used for two purposes. The first being an acknowledgment that all information is true and complete. The second is the authorization of the release of credit and employment history.

b) Percentage of bank account assets attributable toward a loan application

Assets in a bank account are liquid and are therefore attributable toward costs incurred for a loan. Often the lender will prefer that this money is seasoned, meaning it has been in the account for more than 60 days. This is in place to prevent the use of unproperly sourced funds which seemingly appears suddenly.

c) Verifying employment

Ensuring an applicant is employed is a key component in underwriting. Methods of verification include:

- Paystubs
- Background checks
- Contacting the employer

Since a lender cannot verify the employment status of a self-employed individual through a company, they need to see the history of income and determine if it is viable and likely to continue. This can be done most often by reviewing the tax return.

4. Suitability of products & programs – reflecting the type of loan on a mortgage application

The loan application shall indicate the type of loan applied for whether it be conventional, FHA, USDA, VA, or other. Also, the application shall include the loan amount, term, and amortization type.

5. Accuracy (tolerances):

a) Violation scenarios

TILA-RESPA Integrated Disclosure Rule has 3 types of tolerance thresholds. This is to ensure a good faith standard of estimates and to allow the borrower to prepare for the required fees. The three types are:

- Zero tolerance: As the name implies there may be no increase from estimate to closing disclosure
- 10% cumulative tolerance: The change in all fees must not be more than 10%
- No or unlimited tolerance: Any change is acceptable

b) Zero tolerance service charges

Zero tolerance charges shall not change. These charges include:

- Fees paid to the creditor, mortgage broker, or an affiliate
- Fees paid to an unaffiliated third party if the consumer was not allowed to shop
- Transfer taxes

c) 10% tolerance service charges

The 10% tolerance is a cumulation of all the fees. Fees subject to this are:

- All recording fees
- Third-party service fees which the borrower can shop for

6. Disclosure timing:

a) "Know Before You Owe"

The special information pamphlet is a part of the initially required disclosures and must be provided within 3 days of the application. If the applicant is denied within the 3 days, the pamphlet does not need to be provided. If the applicant is denied after the 3 days, the pamphlet needs to be provided within the 3-day window.

b) Notification of action taken

Notice from a creditor to the applicant of adverse action taken must be provided within 30 days after receipt of the credit application. The notice shall include the reason for adverse action whether it be incomplete information or otherwise. The applicant then has 60 days after the time of notice to obtain additional details if requested

c) Early disclosures

The initial disclosures time period begins on the business day following the receipt of the application. The initial disclosures must be provided no later than 3 business days after receipt.

d) Affiliated business arrangements

If required this document must be provided no later than the time of each referral or if a lender specific provider is used, no later than the time of the loan application.

7. Loan estimate timing:

a) Initial Loan Estimate

The loan estimate must be provided no more than three business days after the lender receives the loan application.

The loan estimate need not be provided if the loan is one of the exceptions that do not fall under the TRID or in scenarios where the applicant has waived their right to receive one.

b) Revised Loan Estimate

If the loan estimate needs to be revised, it must be reissued no less than 7 days from loan consummation.

c) Expiration of Loan Estimate settlement charges

The loan estimate expires 10 days after issued to the borrower if a notice of intent to proceed is not provided.

d) Tolerance corrections

If the tolerance corrections exceed the limits, it triggers a revised loan estimate to be provided. This begins a new timeline for review of the revised LE.

8. Closing Disclosure

a) Homeownership Counseling Disclosure

The Dodd-Frank Wall Street Reform and Consumer Protection Act included a requirement that mortgage lenders provide applicants with a list of local housing counselors. The services are to be used to support the borrower to improve financial literacy, expand homeownership opportunities, improve access to affordable housing, and preserve homeownership.

B. Qualification: Processing & Underwriting

1. Borrower Analysis:

a) Assets

Not all assets are considered similarly in their ability to be used for loans. The most common types of assets which are allowed includes:

- Earnest money deposit
- Checking or savings account
- Business accounts
- Stocks

- Bonds
- Mutual funds
- 401k or other retirement funds (to a certain percentage)
- Acceptable gifts
- Sale of assets
- Verified deposits

Some assets which are not acceptable include:

- Cash on hand
- Sweat equity (except in certain circumstances)
- Lender contributions
- Unvested funds
- Undocumented funds
- Illegally obtained funds

Assets can be classified into one of the following categories:

Current Assets: Those which can be easily converted into cash and cash equivalents (typically within a year). Current assets are also termed liquid assets. These include:

- Cash
- Cash equivalents
- Stocks
- Securities

Fixed or Non-Current Assets: Those that cannot be easily and readily converted into cash and cash equivalents. Non-current assets are also termed fixed assets, long-term assets, or hard assets. These include:

- Property
- Buildings
- Machinery
- Equipment
- Patents
- Trademarks

In addition to the costs of obtaining a loan, a lender may require the borrower to have reserve funds available after the transaction occurs. This may include a specific number of months in reserve. The reserve funds are often required to be highly liquid. Due to the early withdrawal penalties and taxes associated with a retirement account, they cannot be considered entirely liquid when evaluating an applicant's reserves.

There may be instances where the lender will require a verification of deposits. In this case, the verification may not come from the borrower. The request shall be sent directly to the depository institution and they also must send the information directly back to the lender.

b) Liabilities

Liabilities are all financial obligations a borrower has established along with the payments of the loan itself. The liabilities listed on form 1003 include:

- All monthly loan payments (auto, student, credit cards, etc.)
- Alimony
- Child support
- Other paycheck deductions such as union dues

There are three types of liabilities:

- Short-term: Due and payable within one year
- Long-term liability: Due and payable beyond one year
- Contingent liabilities: debts that may or may not need to be paid contingent on some conditions

c) Income

Self-employed applicants may have more trouble than others getting approved for a loan. Underwriters will consider taxable income for the basis of consideration and sometimes due to the deductions of self-employed individuals, it can be heavily reduced.

Typically, 24 months of tax return information is required for consideration of a self-employed applicant. In some cases, 12 months can be acceptable if there is previous experience in the same field. Additional documentation may be requested to ensure assets or large deposits were provided from an acceptable source.

Capital gains as income can often be difficult to prove sustainability. Because of this, documentation is required for three consecutive years and must be shown on the tax returns. In addition, a year to date breakdown of capital gains shall be provided.

The underwriter has the ability to review with discretion, but typically the three years are averaged to determine an acceptable monthly income. A history of wild fluctuations or declining gains may cause a lower than average determination.

Acceptable income with proper documentation includes:

- Employment income
- Self-employment income
- Military income
- Social Security or pension
- Non-taxable income
- Rental property income
- Investment income
- Side income

Social Security is a viable source of income for mortgages. All income from the Social Security Administration (SSA) is eligible including Supplemental Security Income (SSI), Social Security Disability Insurance (SSDI), and Social Security Income. The income is evaluated on its verification and likelihood to continue for at least a three-year period. Verification may occur from:

- Tax returns
- Bank statements
- Proof of income letter from SSA
- Social Security Benefit statement

Lenders often require a 2-year employment history. If there is a gap in employment, they may require additional information including a letter of explanation. Typically, underwriters may require the following:

- If there is a gap of six or more months, then they need to be with a full-time job for at least six months to qualify for a mortgage loan.
- If the gaps are less than six months, then they can qualify for a mortgage with verification of the current job

Monthly income must be calculated by taking the yearly salary and dividing it by 12. This may seem to be the same as taking a month's worth of paychecks and multiplying by 12, but not every month has an equal amount of pay. If an hourly rate is provided you can find the monthly salary by:

$$Monthly\ Income = \left(\frac{Hourly\ rate\ x\ Hour\ worked\ per\ week\ x\ 52}{12}\right)$$

d) Credit report

Credit reports include four types of information:

- Bankruptcy and past due accounts
- Information about any credit inquiries
- Credit accounts and details
- Identifying information

To give the consumer the ability to shop around for the best mortgage, the credit report must group credit checks as a single inquiry for 45 days.

Five main factors go into consideration for determining a credit score:

- Bill payment history: Paying bills on time. This accounts for 35% of the score
- Debt Level: This is the ratio of credit debt to the credit limit. This accounts for 30%
- Credit history age: Older credit accounts are considered more reliable than newer ones. This accounts for 15%
- Type of credit: Credit can either be revolving or installment loans. This account for 10%
- Number of inquiries: Too many inquiries in a short period of time is not a desirable factor. Inquires older than 12 months do not have an effect. This accounts for 10%

Consumers who believe there is an issue with credit reports must report the item in question to the credit agencies as soon as possible. Considering this information has a strong impact on an applicant's approval, it is important for it to be accurate. The Fair Credit Reporting Act (FCRA) covers the rights of consumers as it relates to their credit history and provides protection in case of discrepancies. An applicant may submit in writing any errors they believe are present and the credit reporting company must investigate and respond within 30 days.

e) Qualifying ratios (LTV, debt-to-income)

Capacity is the evaluation of a borrower's potential ability-to-repay by considering the comparison of all income to liabilities and the associated ratios. This includes the housing ratio and the back-end ratio.

The housing expense ratio is the percentage of gross monthly income that is devoted to monthly housing expenses.

Loan to value ratio is simply the amount financed divided by the value of the home as determined either by the sale price for a purchase transaction or the appraised value for a refinance:

$$LTV = \frac{Amount\ of\ Loan}{Value\ of\ Property}$$

The debt-to-income ratio is the amount of monthly obligations for a borrower including the mortgage payment to the monthly income:

$$DTI = \frac{(Mortgage + Debt\ Payments)}{Monthly\ Income}$$

The housing-to-income ratio also known as the front-end ratio is an evaluation of income relative to only the proposed total mortgage payment. This includes principal, interest, taxes, hazard insurance, and PMI if applicable. Often the desirable front-end is 28%.

The total debt ratio is also referred to as the back-end ratio. This is the ratio of all proposed monthly obligations including the total mortgage payment and any others to the monthly income. This may include loans, credit cards, or other debts. A favorable back-end ratio is typically considered to be 36% but can be as high as 50% in some circumstances.

f) Ability to repay

The ability to repay rule is mostly centered around 8 factors:

- Current or expected income
- Employment status
- Mortgage payment
- Any additional loans secured by the same property
- Property taxes, insurance, and any other associated costs related to the property
- Monthly debts
- Debt-to-income ratios
- Credit history

Income must be proven and shown to reasonably continue. Most often the W-2's, tax returns, and paystubs are the best representation of this and often a minimum of the 2 most recent is required to be provided. There are other methods which are less common:

- Employer letter
- Bank statements
- Social Security statements
- Annuity statements
- Pension statement

Assets are also required to be verified and can be considered in the following accounts:

- Checking
- Savings
- CDs
- Stocks
- Mutual funds
- Bonds
- Retirement accounts

Often the assets available may need to be seasoned which means they have been in the account for 60 days. Cash can also be used but must also often be seasoned to be considered verified.

Lenders must investigate, consider, and document the borrower's income, assets, employment, and credit history. This must be complied with to follow the ability-to-replay rule. The lender will evaluate the applicant on all of the factors and make a determination based on the perceived risk of the transaction.

The allowable DTI ratio will vary from lender to lender. The qualified mortgage rule sets a maximum at 43%, but lenders may choose to set this lower to around 40% or higher to 50% if they see reason to do so. It is very uncommon for the DTI's to be above 50%. FHA has separate requirements and sets the front-end limit at 31% and the back-end at 43%. VA loans often have a back-end maximum of 41%.

Safe Harbor is a legal protection to lenders that are associated with qualified loans. If a borrower that defaults elects to sue the borrower, the lender is protected under the ability to repay rule and this is a strong legal defense.

An evaluation of a net tangible benefit determines if the benefits of a transaction outweigh the costs. It is used to prevent against borrowers taking out loans or refinancing that is not in their best interest as shown through the numbers.

For example, in a refinance transaction, there are fees associated with the benefit of receiving a better interest rate. The borrower also likely will have a different loan term which may be longer or shorter. The borrower will want to look at when the savings will exceed the costs of the transaction by saving interest over a period of time. The determinization of acceptable benefit is not exact and there is an associated perception, but all factors must be considered to weight the proposed benefit of a transaction.

2. Appraisals:

a) Purpose/definitions

Appraisals are a third-party, independent evaluation of a home. They are always involved in a purchase transaction and are likely included in refinancing or other non-purchase transactions. The appraisal is necessary to ensure that the lender is not providing more money to the borrower for the loan than the asset is worth. This way in case of default, the asset can account for the remaining balance. If an appraisal comes in at less than the proposed transaction loan amount, then the transaction will not be processed unless the borrower provides a greater down payment. There are three types of appraisals which will be discussed in the following sections.

b) Approaches (market, income, cost)

The market approach is the most common of the appraisal types and is used for most purchase loans. The value of the home is determined by comparison to other properties with similar characteristics that have been sold in as recent of a timeframe as possible. The comparisons (referred to as "comps") are then evaluated by identifying the differences in certain characteristics such as square footage, age, lot size, home type, street type, and many others. Typically, a minimum of three comps are required, and the most similar and most recent homes are chosen. At times, homes that are currently on the market are also used as a basis for comparison but will not hold as much weight as the sales. If possible, homes no more than a 1-mile radius away from the home shall be chosen and as well as no more than 1 year prior to the transaction.

Once the comps are evaluated in comparison to the home to be purchased, the prices of the sales are adjusted to represent a price of equal value. These values are then averaged and evaluated using some appraiser judgment to determine a fair market value of the home.

The income approach is a way of evaluating investment properties that will generate income. This is common for condo or apartment complexes where renters will reside. The approach involves calculating the Net Operating Income (NOI), which is the income generated divided by the capitalization rate:

$$NOI = \frac{Income}{Capitalization\ Rate}$$

The capitalization rate is a percentage representation of the expected income that can be generated from a property on a yearly basis if it is bought with a cash investment.

For a building that is not frequently sold, the cost approach determines what the value of the property may be by assuming that a reasonable buyer would not pay more than for a comparable building on a comparable lot. Often this is most appropriate for buildings such as schools, hospitals, or government buildings that are not bought and sold frequently.

Choosing comparable properties does not have exact requirements but should be as close as possible in size, location, age, and other characteristics. The comparable homes should also be sold as recently as possible. Homes shall also not be sold longer than a year from the proposed transaction. In rural areas, a lower volume of sales may lead to an expansion of the requirements for the chosen comparable properties. The appraiser shall use sound judgment based on the market to choose the most appropriate homes.

c) Timing

The ECOA Valuations Rule provides requirements for a borrower's right to receive an appraisal. The borrower must be provided with a disclosure that includes the following:

- Notice that the applicant has the right to receive an appraisal report.
- Notice that the request must be in writing.
- Providing the lender's mailing address.
- The lender must send a copy of the appraisal report as long as they receive the request less than 90 days after the notice of action taken is provided.

The lender is required to send the right to receive a copy of the appraisal disclosure no more than 3 days from the date of application.

d) Independent appraisal requirement

The appraiser must provide accurate and impartial evaluations of the properties involved in transactions. The appraiser must not be influenced by any involved in the transaction to sway the value of the property in a direction that is in a specific party's best interests. However, unbiased additional information may be provided to the appraiser for consideration. This may occur if the lender or borrower discovers missing or incorrect information on an appraisal, which may impact the valuation.

3. Title Report:

a) Obtaining title reports

The title report may be obtained through any means desired by the purchaser. It can be done personally at the assessor's office or courthouse but most often it is obtained through a professional.

b) Timing of title reports and commitments

The title report and any commitments must be obtained before closing on the property. A typical timeframe of the search is around two weeks but can take much longer depending on the property.

c) Preliminary title reports

A preliminary title report is used to see if there may be complications that can arise when the title is transferred. This may include things such as liens on the property or outstanding taxes.

4. Insurance:

a) Flood insurance

Flood insurance is an additional aspect of hazard insurance for certain properties. FEMA requirements stipulate that the flood coverage must be at least the lesser of:

- The maximum amount of NFIP coverage available for the particular property type, or
- The outstanding principal balance of the loan, or
- The insurable value of the structure.

The requirement for flood insurance is determined by the location of the property and whether or not they are in the specific designated flood zones. The Flood Emergency Management Agency (FEMA) provides the flood zone maps. Flood insurance is required in high-risk areas designated as Zone A and Zone V.

The amount of flood insurance is determined by the type of property and the limits of the property. The minimum amount of flood insurance is the least of the following three:

- The National Flood Insurance Program (NFIP) Maximum
- The insurable value of the property
- The loan amount

NFIP typically cannot exceed $250,000 for the structure of the home and $100,000 for personal property

Private flood insurance can also be purchased to satisfy the requirements. The advantage is the limits on private insurance are much higher than the maximums provided by NFIP. The private flood insurance cost is a function of the FEMA hazard area. The more high-risk area, the higher the cost.

If there is no insurance on a property due to reasons such as failure to pay, the lender can force insurance on the borrower so that the property is still protected. This is known as force-placed insurance.

b) PMI

Private Mortgage Insurance (PMI) is protection for the lender. The borrower pays a monthly fee that is used to insure the lender in the event of default.

While PMI does not cover the borrower in the event of default, it helps the lender to have more confidence in the borrower's ability to repay. This has allowed less qualified borrowers to get loans, especially in the case of lower down payment amounts.

The yearly cost of PMI is typically between 0.5% to 1.0% of the total loan amount. This yearly cost is divided into equal monthly payments as a part of the borrower's monthly obligations. The amount is often a function of the down payment amount. The more put down, the less the yearly premium will be.

FHA loans will also require an initial premium cost for the loan called an upfront mortgage insurance premium. This does not replace the need for monthly PMI payments as a part of the loan but provides extra insurance due to the low required down payment.

One of the many benefits of VA loans is they do not require PMI.

If the initial down payment is less than 20%, PMI will end automatically at a scheduled LTV of 78%. This also holds true if extra payments are applied to the principal despite the fact that a loan may have the necessary equity to remove PMI there is a seasoning period in which the borrower must wait to apply to remove the payment. This period is a minimum of 2 years.

PMI is required if the loan to value ratio is greater than 80%. If 80% is not achieved, the PMI will automatically be stopped at an LTV of 78% in accordance with the amortization schedule. A borrower can apply to have PMI removed a minimum of 2 years after the origination of the loan if there is reason to believe the loan to value has decreased. This may be because of principal payoff or an increased appraisal.

c) Hazard/homeowner insurance

The hazard insurance must show that it fully covers damage from natural occurrences. This may include an endorsement or separate policy from the original. The claims must be settled however on a replacement cost basis and not actual value.

d) Government mortgage insurance

Mortgage insurance can be either private (PMI) or government backed by an agency such as the Federal Housing Authority (FHA). This insurance still covers the lender in the case of default in the same way private insurance does.

C. Closing

1. Title and title insurance

The title insurance covers both the lender and the borrower from loss or damages resulting from the property title. This may be existing liens or encumbrances that will result in financial attention. Unlike typical insurance, this insurance covers past events that have not yet been uncovered.

Priority in the case of multiple mortgages is determined by a subordination agreement to establish the hierarchy of loans. Junior liens are established and are only paid after the primary loans have been paid in the case of default.

An easement is the granting of rights to use or access land. Easements are important to be made aware of during a purchase transaction as there can be a misrepresentation of the acceptable use of a piece of land by other parties. Easements can be both permanent or temporary.

An encumbrance is a restriction on a property that may restrict the sale of the property. This may include:

- Liens
- Deed restrictions
- Easements
- Encroachments
- Licenses

Reconveyance transfers the property title from one entity to another. This is common when the loan has been paid off in full. The deed of reconveyance is a notification that the borrower has been released of the obligation of debt.

2. Settlement/Closing Agent:

a) Eligible signatures on security instrument

The security instrument must be signed by the following:

- Each person who has an ownership interest in the property
- The spouse or domestic partner of any person who has an ownership interest in the property

b) Power of attorney

A power of attorney may be used to allow a specified agent to sign documents on the borrower or seller's behalf. This must be established by a notarized power of attorney form in the county in which the property for the transaction resides.

3. Explanation of fees – HUD-1, title insurance, pre-paids, escrow expenses, loan origination fees

The settlement statement is a summary to identify all details costs and fees for the transaction. Fees and charges listed include:

- Broker/sales commissions
- Origination fee
- Loan discount
- Appraisal fee
- Credit report fee
- Lender's inspection fee
- Mortgage insurance application fee
- Assumption fee
- Items to be paid in advance
    - Taxes
    - Interest
    - Insurance
- Escrow reserves
- Title charges
- Recording and transfer fees
- Any additional fees not listed

Title insurance is paid as a one-time fee upfront and varies based on the value of the property and the anticipated work to secure the necessary title information.

Prepaids are payments that are required to be provided before they are due to the appropriate entity. Generally, for mortgages, this refers to the funding of escrow accounts including the property taxes, hazard insurance, and PMI. Lenders will often require that the escrow account includes a minimum amount of reserves to ensure there are sufficient funds in the account. The prepaids will include this buffer along with the required amount that will be needed at the time the bill is due.

At closing, there are often expenses related to establishing the escrow account. Generally, the funding of escrow accounts includes property taxes, hazard insurance, and PMI. Lenders will often require that the escrow account includes a minimum amount of reserves to ensure there are sufficient funds in the account. The prepaids will include this buffer along with the required amount that will be needed at the time the bill is due.

Origination fees are often a percentage of the purchase price, typically 1%. However, this can vary and there are instances where it is waived in return for a higher interest rate, in which case the fee is paid by means of the yield spread premium.

4. Required closing documents

Documents to be provided at closing must include:

- Closing Disclosure (CD)
- Promissory Note
- Mortgage/Security Instrument/Deed of Trust
- Transfer of ownership for purchase transactions
- Right to Cancel
- Escrow statement

For a property to be used as collateral certain stipulations must apply and appropriate documentation shall be provided. The property must be free and clear of liens and have enough equity to cover the loan amount. Some documentation required includes:

- Proof of ownership (deed)
- Notice of satisfaction of mortgage
- Insurance declarations
- Property valuation (typically an appraisal)

The mortgage note legally binds the borrower to repaying the loan. It covers:

- The amount owed
- Interest rate
- Payment due dates
- Lifetime total amount of the loan
- Loan term
- Allowable changes to the monthly payment
- Where to send payments
- Actions taken if payment is not made.

Certain circumstances cause a lender to include an acceleration clause into a loan. This allows the lender to require the borrower to repay the entirety of the existing loan when requested even before the endpoint of the loan term. This is also referred to often as an "acceleration covenant". The lender will impose stipulations in the agreement of the loan, which if met, will allow the lender to request the acceleration payment. Most commonly this is triggered by delinquent payments but can be for other reasons such as transference of property ownership.

5. Funding – rescission periods

A rescission period is the time the borrower is allowed to cancel the transaction. It does not officially begin however until all of the following are provided:

- Credit contract is signed (usually known as the Promissory Note)
- A Truth in Lending disclosure is provided
- Two copies of a notice explaining the right to rescind are provided

Once all of these are provided, a three-business day period begins. The first day after the last item is provided counts as day 1.

The bank or lender cannot fund the loan until the rescission period is complete. All fees are refundable with the exception of any third-party costs.

D. Financial Calculations

1. Periodic interest

A periodic interest rate calculates interest based on the number of compounding periods. Lenders will typically quote interest rates based on an annual basis, but the compounding of the interest occurs most often at a monthly interval. This means that interest is being calculated at a rate of the annual divided by the number of compounding periods in a year. Be sure to convert the interest rate to decimal form by dividing by 100:

$$Interest = \frac{Rate\ in\ decimal\ form}{\#\ of\ compunding\ periods} \times Principal\ Balance$$

Most often mortgages compound once per month or 12 times per year. So, the interest rate is divided by 12 to find the monthly interest.

Some important notes to remember about periodic interest:

- Lenders most often quote interest rates on an annual basis, but the interest compounds more frequently than annually in most cases.
- The interest rate and the APR are not often the same number
- The more frequently a loan compounds, the quicker it grows, or in the case of mortgages, the more interest is paid over the life of the loan

Interest per diem by definition is a calculation of interest on a per-day basis as opposed to monthly. This means that interest accumulates every day, and therefore there is a slight difference in typical monthly interest calculations:

$$Daily\ Interest\ for\ a\ Monthly\ Payment = \frac{rate}{365} \times pricipal \times number\ of\ days$$

2. Monthly payments

The monthly payment is a combination of the principal and interest payment plus any required monthly escrow contributions:

$$Total\ monthly\ mortgage\ payment$$
$$= Principal + Interest + Property\ Tax + Hazard\ insurance + PMI\ (If\ applicable)$$

3. Down payments

Down payments are the amount of money provided by the borrower to make an initial payment against a loan. To calculate the down payment percentage, divide the amount of the down payment by the purchase price. Be careful to not use the loan amount:

$$\%\ Down\ Payment = \frac{Down\ Payment}{Purchase\ Price}$$

4. Closing costs/prepaids

Closing costs include the expenses beyond the cost of the property itself that it takes to get the loan. Typically closing costs will range from 2%-5% of the purchase price of a loan.

5. ARM adjustments – interest rates and payments

The fully indexed rate is the addition of the fixed margin rate and the variable index rate as determined by the agreed-upon index. The rate must not exceed the lifetime cap or the adjustment period cap:

$$Fully\ Indexed\ Rate = Margin + Index$$

The monthly payment for an adjustable-rate mortgage shall adjust based on the changes in the property tax and hazard insurance similarly to a fixed-rate mortgage. In addition, the monthly payment may change as the rate adjusts up or down due to the change in the fully indexed rate.

V. Ethics (18%)

A. Ethical Issues

1. Prohibited acts:

a) Redlining

Redlining is the unethical practice of not providing services to residents of a certain area based on race or ethnicity. This may include not lending money to a person of a specific race or not showing properties in a specific community to certain people.

b) RESPA prohibitions

RESPA covers prohibitions in sections 8, 9, and 10:

- Section 8 of RESPA prohibits kickbacks, fee-splitting, and unearned fees.

- Section 9 of RESPA prohibits home sellers from requiring buyers to purchase their settlement services from a particular company as a requirement of sale.

- Section 10 of RESPA provides escrow prohibitions including the amount required in the account for the payment of taxes, hazard insurance, and other charges.

c) Kickbacks/compensation

Kickbacks are compensation paid illegally to an individual involved in a real estate transaction so that they may provide a specific recommendation, service, or decision. This would be an MLO being paid by a third-party service to be recommended.

d) Permitted/prohibited duties

The loan processor provides the final approval of a loan application before going to the lender. They will check for red flags and ensure all information is verifiable done accurately. They may not offer or negotiate loan terms. This must be done by a properly licensed individual.

2. Fairness in lending:

a) Referral (Definition/required disclosures)

A referral is not necessarily a violation of RESPA Section 8 as long as there is not a requirement to use the specified company. The referral should be accompanied by an affiliated business disclosure. This disclosure must include the details of the relationship and the estimate for the service. It shall be provided at the time of the referral and no later.

b) Coercion

Coercion is the act of trying to persuade someone to act involuntarily in the best interest of a specific party. In reals estate transactions this can occur in any scenario during the process where there is something to be gained. As an example, this can occur with appraisers who may provide a home value below a required mark in the best interest of a specific party.

c) Appraiser conflict of interest

A conflict of interest occurs when the appraiser has lost the ability to provide a fully independent and unbiased opinion. The perception or appearance of a conflict is enough for the appraisal to be compromised.

One scenario where there is a conflict is simultaneous obligation. This is where an appraiser is in a situation where two parties are represented. For example, this can occur during a matrimonial dispute.

Another conflict may occur when an appraiser is asked to provide services on the same property for a different client. This may put undue pressure on the appraiser to adhere to the previous numbers.

d) Discrimination/fairness

Discrimination in lending shall not be tolerated. Applicants must have an equal opportunity to receive loans and to be treated fairly. Discrimination is prohibited as a part of:

- Fair Housing Act
- Civil Rights Act
- Home Mortgage Disclosure Act
- The Community Reinvestment Act

All applicants must receive the same level of treatment in a fair and just manner. Examples of unfair treatment include:

- Refusing to provide a loan
- Refusing to provide loan information
- Appraisal discrimination
- Imposing different terms or conditions on different people

3. Fraud detection:

a) Asset/income/employment fraud

Asset fraud is a misrepresentation of assets to obtain a loan. The possible fraud indications can include:

- Asset Documentation
- Salary does not match deposits
- Nontraditional banking institutions
- Inconsistent dates of bank statements
- No paper-trail for funds
- Unknown related parties

Employment and income documentation red flags include:

- Generic job title
- Home address excessively far from employer without remote employment
- Employer not responsive
- Paychecks not matching deposits
- Abuse of overtime

b) Sales contract/application red flags

Fannie Mae provides guidance on the potentially troubling aspects of a contract during review. Sales contract red flags include:

- Seller not on the title
- Purchaser name is different than the application name
- There is no real estate agent involved in the transaction
- Power of attorney
- Earnest money is the entirety of the down payment

- More than one deposit checks
- Unusual real estate agent commission

Mortgage Application indicators include:

- Significant changes from original application to the subsequent
- Unsigned or undated application
- P.O. Box or unclear employer address
- Loan is a cash-out refinance on a recently acquired property
- Payment shock
- Purchaser does not own property

c) Occupancy fraud

Occupancy fraud is related to the applicant lying about the home being owner-occupied. An owner-occupied home can often get lower interest rates than investment properties.

d) General red flags

High-level red flag concerns include:

- Social Security number
- Address not matching
- Altered documentations
- Differing handwriting styles
- Automated underwriting submissions are excessive

4. Suspicious bank and other activity; information not provided to borrower; verifying application information

There are two scenarios of fraud regarding the consumer's bank account. The first is fraudulent activity by the consumer and the second being activity taken against the consumer when the account has been compromised.

Activity by the consumer may include:

- Suspicious Cash Transactions
    - Deposits just below the reportable minimum
    - A number of deposits over a period of time below the reportable minimum
    - Suspicious transactions

- Check tampering
- Billing such as unexplainable reimbursements or fees

Fraud activity against the consumer can happen when the account has been compromised either by obtaining the consumer's personal information or by theft. These are usually identified by unusual transactions in different locations than the consumer is in.

There is a wide range of required disclosure for numerous steps throughout the mortgage process. The consumers have rights by regulations to be provided all of the necessary disclosures and information. If not, the party is in violation of federal codes and is subject to penalties.

Liability fraud protects against fraudulent activity that may occur on accounts. It releases the consumer of any liability on unauthorized uses of credit.

Loan originators are required to report any suspicious activity that could jeopardize both the lender's investment and the applicant's wellbeing. If a financial institution suspects suspicious or illegal behavior, they must file a Suspicious Activity Report (SAR).

Documentation and consistency are the keys to an underwriter verifying the information provided on an application is accurate as stated by the applicant. The amounts of income, assets, and liabilities shall be consistent across all bank statements, paystubs, accounts, and any other documentation.

Verification of gray areas may even be taken a step further. Certain actions that may be taken include contacting an employer to verify employment status or asking the applicant for a Letter of Explanation to provide further information and documentation on a questionable aspect of the application.

5. Advertising:

a) Misleading information

It is prohibited to provide advertising which includes misrepresentations, expressly or by implication, in any commercial communication regarding any term of any mortgage. Regulation N prohibits misrepresentations or misleading claims in advertising. As per section 1014.3, this includes among others:

- Type and amount of mortgage fees
- Terms, payments, or amount of loan
- Taxes or insurance associated with a loan

- Type of mortgage
- Interest rate details
- Misrepresentations of the source of commercial communication
- Ability of a consumer to be approved for a loan

When an attractive product is presented to get a potential customer engaged but then is sold a different product, this is a bait and switch. This is a prohibited practice and any advertised product must be actually available to the consumer.

b) Due diligence review

It is required that advertisements are reviewed for compliance before publication. They should be reviewed to ensure they are truthful and clearly state the ability for terms and conditions to change. Products advertised must be actually available to the consumer. Negligence is not an excuse for unlawful advertising.

c) "Unfair, deceptive, or abusive acts"

It is prohibited to provide advertising which includes misrepresentations, expressly or by implication, in any commercial communication regarding any term of any mortgage.

d) Federal regulation

Federal regulations apply to any loans which fall under the definition of commercial communication. This in brief can be described as any written or oral statement, illustration or depiction, in any language, that is designed to create interest in a good or service. It may appear in any label, package, television, print, and many other forms.

6. Predatory lending and steering

Steering is forcing a specific geographical area on an applicant based on race, religion, or ethnicity, and it is strictly prohibited.

Loan types must be clearly and properly designated so that the consumer is not misled into thinking a product is available or obtainable that is not.

B. Ethical behavior related to loan origination activities

1. Financial responsibility:

a) Permitted fees/compensation; fee changes; closing cost scenarios; referral fees; fee splitting

Permitted fees which are for services actually rendered and not based on a referral include:

- Payment to an attorney
- Payment to a title agent for title insurance
- A lender payment to its suitably appointed agent or contractor for services actually performed
- A bona fide salary or payment for goods or services actually performed
- An employer's payment to its own employees for referral services

A changed circumstance as defined earlier is an acceptable reason for numbers to change on a loan estimate. Fees that have been paid already such as third-party services will not change.

Fees from the loan estimate to the closing disclosure are evaluated based on what threshold they are allowed to increase by. They can be zero tolerance, 10% tolerance, or no tolerance.

Closing costs and changes related to them fall under three categories:

- Costs that can be increased without restriction
- Costs that can be increased up to a specific threshold (10% in most cases)
- Costs that may not be increased at all

The exception to this is in the event of a change in circumstances in which a re-evaluation of fees is determined.

Missing funds at settlement must be resolved before the transaction can be completed. The mortgage company may withhold funds until the transaction is completed or a debt is settled. For instance, if an existing lien which was to be paid at settlement has not cleared the payment yet, funds can be withheld until this transaction is complete.

A referral is any written or oral action directed to a person that affects or influences the selection of a settlement service provider. Under RESPA, it is illegal to pay or receive a fee to refer settlement services to a particular person or business. For example, a mortgage lender may not pay a real estate broker for referring an individual to the lender.

Fee splitting occurs when there is an agreement of a sharing of a fee for a settlement service if a referral is provided. Fee splitting is prohibited under RESPA.

2. Handling borrower complaints

CFPB receives and handles consumer complaints. Complaints are collected and then forwarded to the company in question for a response. The process for complaints will proceed as follows:

- Complaint is submitted by the consumer and received by CFPB for screening
- CFPB investigates the complaint for a legitimate existing or prior business relationship. Where none is found, the complaint is dismissed.
- Complaint is then sent to the company in question.
- The company shall respond within 30 days or CFPB addresses the concern with a consumer response team.

There are three rules as established by the Gramm-Leach Bliley Act:

- The Financial Privacy Rule: Requires providing customers with privacy disclosures
- Safeguard Rule: Requires written security plans by institutions to protect consumer information
- Pretexting Prohibition: Prohibits the practice of collecting information under false pretenses

3. Mortgage company compliance:

a) Discovery of material information; information supplied by employers

An MLO has a legal and ethical responsibility to provide any adverse information immediately upon discovery to the lender, which may be evidence of a violation of regulations or an indication of misrepresentation.

Mortgage lenders will gather information from employers to verify employment. The ability to make contact comes from consent by the applicant. The information is typically obtained by directly calling the company to verify items such as income, position, and longevity of the position.

MLO's are responsible for ethical and compliant practice and shall inform lenders of any information which is necessary to the evaluation of the applicant. Withholding information of any kind will result in penalties.

4. Relationships with consumers:

a) Handling personal information/cybersecurity; disclosing conflicts of interest; requesting credit reports

The MLO is in a privileged position in regard to knowledge of specific information about the client. Any personal information that is provided in any means shall be kept confidential. Personal information shall only be used for the purposes of business and its specific intention. The sharing of information with anyone including family members is strictly prohibited. The use of confidential information must also not be used in any way for personal gain. This confidentiality applies to anytime during and after the loan process.

FCRA provides limitations on when a credit report can be accessed without written consent from the consumer. These include those who have a current or potential relationship with the consumer, such as a landlord, utility company, employer, or insurance company. FCRA also provides other instances where it is permissible for credit to be pulled:

- When credit is applied for
- Application for insurance
- When a creditor intends to extend credit
- Employment-related scenarios with the consent of the applicant
- Court-ordered
- Government benefits or licensure applications
- Any "legitimate business need" for a business transaction

Disclosure of information is a large part of ethical compliance. MLO's are required to disclose any conflicts of interest related to any transactions. These disclosures include:

- Outside business relationships
- Personal relationships related to the transactions
- Prior employment relationships
- Any financial interests

Proper steps shall be taken to ensure the most secure transactions and interactions can occur. Financial institutions and employees in the mortgage field must be aware of the dangers online, especially when dealing with sensitive information. Some precautions include:

- Cybersecurity systems
- Regular security testing
- Backup systems
- Data encryptions

- Formal security incident protocols
- Data monitoring
- Identification of all hardware and software used on the system
- Restoration plans

Any personal information that is provided in any means shall be kept confidential. Personal information shall only be used for the purposes of business and its specific intention. The sharing of information with anyone including family members is strictly prohibited. The use of confidential information must also not be used in any way for personal gain. This confidentiality applies for any time during and after the loan process.

Mortgage lenders may investigate any information that they feel has an impact on the applicant's ability to repay the loan. They are not allowed to ask about anything related to family planning or health. As an example, they may not be biased against a woman who will become pregnant and take maternity leave. They may also not incorporate the health of an applicant into their ability to earn an income.

b) Changes in down payments or offered interest rates; powers of attorney; non-resident coborrowers

The expectations of the amount of a required down payment must not be deceptive in any way. If there is reason for the consumer to believe they are only required to provide a certain amount, such as 0% money down, they must be informed of any other costs or fees in the estimated final requirements

Similarly, to down payment amounts, the consumer shall not be led to believe that the interest rate will be a specific amount, without proper disclosures of the adjustability. These scenarios shall not include an omission of material fact. Material fact can be defined as any information which if known, might have reasonably caused the consumer to make a different choice.

A power of attorney may be used to allow a specified agent to sign documents on the borrower or seller's behalf. This must be established by a notarized power of attorney form in the county in which the property for the transaction resides. The power of attorney shall not be compelled in any way against their will to act in manner that is not in the interest of the represented party.

A co-borrower is a second individual on an application whose income, assets, and credit history are also taken into consideration for the underwriting of the loan. The co-borrower is just as liable as the other applicant in the obligations for repaying the loan. Co-borrowers are often used when an individual cannot obtain a specific loan alone. This is not the same as a cosigner. A cosigner is an individual who is responsible for the loan only in the case of default.

c) Unreported/fluctuating income; gifts/unexplained deposits; appraiser interactions; multiple applications

The applicant must provide the appropriate information related to income. However, there are specific situations in which the creditor may not ask the applicant to provide information. These include:

- Alimony
- Child support
- Separate maintenance payments as income

Occasionally an applicant will try to make income appear to be greater than it is for fear of being denied a loan with insufficient income. One method of verification is looking for consistency with deposits and stated income. If there is a discrepancy, this can certainly be considered a red flag for potential misrepresentation. The MLO may request a Letter of Explanation (LOE) in which the applicant explains situations or transactions for better documentation and understanding of the financial situation.

As per Fannie Mae requirements, a donor must be a relative by blood, marriage, adoption, or legal guardian. They may not be the builder, the developer, the real estate agent, or any other interested party to the transaction. The underwriter shall take appropriate measures to verify the authenticity and acceptability of any gift involved in a transaction.

The appraisal needs to be an independent and unbiased evaluation of a property value. The most common violation is the suggestion of a specific value that may advance a transaction. In other words, the appraiser shall in no way be informed of the effect a specific value may have on a transaction.

Applicants have the right to shop around for mortgages and may proceed with multiple lenders at the same time. The borrower is at risk however of double paying for services if they proceed too far into the process.

A borrower shall provide the appropriate information regarding income on an application and have appropriate documentation such as W-2's, tax returns, and paystubs. Income can be more fluid in certain circumstances and the stability may need to be verified. If certain aspects of the income are not clear, the underwriter may ask for a Letter of Explanation (LOE) in which the applicant explains situations or transactions for better documentation and understanding of the financial situation.

d) Truth in marketing and advertising – permissible statements in advertising

Advertisements must not be misleading in any way and be for products which are actually available. Because of this, there are restrictions on what may or may not be stated in an ad. All interest rates, fees, taxes, insurance, prepayment penalties, and other mortgage aspects stated must be truthful. Some specific statements which have requirements include:

- The term "fixed" when used with an adjustable-rate must include the phrase "ARM", "Variable Rate mortgage" or "Adjustable Rate Mortgage". It must also be accompanied by a statement indicating the length of a fixed term.
- The terms "no-cost" and "no-fees"

As stated earlier triggering terms and statements need additional statements associated with them. Triggering terms include:

- A down payment (percentage or amount)
- The number of payments
- The loan term
- A finance charge

Any mentioning of these terms must include as appropriate the following:

- Amount or % of the down payment
- Terms of repayment
- Use of the term "annual percentage rate" and if the rate may be increased

e) General business ethics:

i. Falsified information by borrower or MLO

Falsifying loan application information for the purposes of obtaining a loan may be prosecuted regardless of whether or not the false information resulted in a loss for the financial institution. Federal law requires the discovery of false application information to be reported. The borrower can face significant charges and be prosecuted. Some penalties include seizing of property, licenses being revoked, or even jail time in some cases.

The MLO can face similar charges to that of the borrower when involved in falsifying information on the loan application. The MLO may be charged if they knew and did not address the issue. Penalties can be more severe if the MLO willingly participated in falsifying the application. For penalties, the MLO's license will be revoked at minimum and additional criminal penalties may apply, including fines or jail time.

ii. Giving solicited/unsolicited advice

Advice to the borrower must be provided by those qualified and ethically able to do so. For instance, an MLO should never provide legal advice. This should be done by a qualified lawyer.

The advice provided to a borrower shall not be outside of the licensed individual's scope of duties. Mainly legal advice shall only be given by an appropriate attorney.

iii. Outside parties seeking information

The sharing of information with unauthorized parties is strictly prohibited. The sharing of information must be either approved by written consent by the individual or be a scenario in which information must be provided for legal or regulatory purposes.

Question 1

According to the Real Estate Settlement Procedures Act (RESPA), which of the following statements does not fit the definition of a mortgage broker?

(A) Renders origination services
(B) Serves as an intermediary between borrower and lender
(C) Is an employee of the lender
(D) Involved in transactions including federally related loans

Question 2

According to the Real Estate Settlement Procedures Act (RESPA), what action is not prohibited?

(A) A split, portion, or percentage of services actually performed
(B) Compensation for a referral
(C) An understanding for the referral of business
(D) A promise of payment at a future date

Question 3

According to the Real Estate Settlement Procedures Act (RESPA), Which of the following disclosures is not required to be provided at the time of loan applications?

(A) A Special Information Booklet
(B) An estimate of settlement costs
(C) Initial Escrow Statement
(D) Mortgage Servicing Disclosure statement

Question 4

The Real Estate Settlement Procedures Act (RESPA), typically applies to all of the following except:

(A) Hazard insurance agents
(B) Title companies
(C) Home improvement contractors
(D) Appraisers

Question 5

Within what time frame must an affiliated business disclosure be provided to a client according to RESPA?

(A) At the time of each referral
(B) At the time of the first referral only
(C) Within 24 hours of the referral
(D) Within 7 days of the referral

Question 6

As per the Equal Credit Opportunity Act (ECOA), what is not a permissible scenario in which a creditor can inquire about an applicant's spouse?

(A) The spouse will be able to use the account
(B) The spouse is contractually liable on the account
(C) The spouse's income is used as a basis of repayment
(D) The applicant is providing alimony to the spouse

Question 7

As per ECOA, which statement is not consistent with the definition of adverse action?

(A) A denial of grant credit as requested in an application
(B) An agreed to change in the terms of an account by an applicant
(C) A closing of an account that does not affect all of a class of the creditor's accounts
(D) A denial to increase the amount of credit available

Question 8

As per ECOA, what is not consistent with the requirements regarding the denial of an application?

(A) The principal reason for denial must be disclosed
(B) The specific number of reasons for denial must be disclosed
(C) The specified reasons disclosed must relate to the factors actually considered by the creditor
(D) A creditor may not need to describe how a factor adversely affected the applicant

Question 9

As per the Truth in Lending Act, what is not a disclosure requirement related to providing the right to rescind?

(A) How to exercise the right to rescind
(B) The effects of rescission
(C) A recommendation of potential rescission
(D) The date the rescission period expires

Question 10

As per the TILA, which of the following is not considered a triggering term for advertising which will activate additional requirements?

(A) Rate of finance charge
(B) Amount of down payment
(C) Amount of any payment
(D) Amount of any finance charge

Question 11

As per the TILA, which of the following scenarios would not meet the definition of a standard mortgage for the means of refinancing?

(A) A term of 35 years
(B) A fixed-rate for 2 years and adjustable thereafter
(C) The principal balance does not increase
(D) The repayment of the principal cannot be deferred by the consumer

Question 12

What is the limit of variation for an annual percentage rate?

(A) 1/10 of 1%
(B) 1/8 of 1%
(C) 1/4 of 1%
(D) ½ of 1%

Question 13

Which of the following types of transactions are exempt from HOEPA coverage?

(A) Refinances
(B) Closed-end home equity loan
(C) Purchase-money mortgages
(D) Reverse mortgages

Question 14

According to HOEPA, what is not a circumstance in which balloon payments are allowed for high-cost mortgages?

(A) The payment schedule is adjusted to accommodate irregular income
(B) The loan is a short-term bridge loan
(C) The creditor meets the requirements for serving an underserved area
(D) An additional loan is supplied to cover the outstanding balance at the end of the loan

Question 15

To meet the requirements of qualifying for a high-cost mortgage the transaction's total points and fees must exceed what percentage of the total loan amount if the total is greater than $20,000 adjusted for inflation?

(A) 2%
(B) 5%
(C) 8%
(D) 10%

Question 16

For a subordinate lien, the APR must exceed the APOR for a comparable transaction by what minimum percentage?

(A) 1%
(B) 1.5%
(C) 2.5%
(D) 3.5%

Question 17

What type of data below is excluded from being reported by a financial institution as a part of the Home Mortgage Disclosure Act?

(A) Data about ethnicity
(B) Loans on unimproved land
(C) The type of loan
(D) Loans for home improvement

Question 18

According to the Fair Credit Reporting Act (FCRA), who may initiate a fraud alert?

(A) The direct consumer only
(B) The direct consumer or family members only
(C) The direct consumer or an individual acting in good faith on the consumer's behalf
(D) The direct consumer or an anonymous source

Question 19

As per the FCRA, what is not a permissible scenario for which a reporting agency can furnish a consumer report to a third-party person?

(A) Credit transactions
(B) Employment purposes
(C) Legal action
(D) Underwriting of insurance

Question 20

According to the Bank Secrecy Act, a financial institution must file a Suspicious Activity Report for all of the following except:

(A) Insider abuse of any amount
(B) Criminal violations of any amount when the suspect can be identified
(C) Criminal violations of $25,000 or more if there is no potential identification
(D) Illegal transactions at or through the financial institution.

Question 21

Before a financial institution can disclose nonpublic information to a third party, what is not a requirement that must be provided to the consumer?

(A) An initial notice of the institution's privacy policies
(B) An opt-out notice
(C) Identification of the third party
(D) A reasonable time frame to opt-out

Question 22

What is the latest permissible time for phone calls from telemarketers?

(A) 7 pm
(B) 8 pm
(C) 9 pm
(D) 10 pm

Question 23

As per Mortgage Acts and Practices how long from the initial date of commercial communication must all documents be kept?

(A) 30 days
(B) 90 days
(C) 12 months
(D) 24 months

Question 24

What is not a minimum requirement for financial institutions in regard to the verification of the identity of a consumer as per the Patriot Act?

(A) Maintain records used for identity verification
(B) Consult lists of known terrorists when evaluating a consumer
(C) Require multiple forms of identification from the consumer
(D) Pursue a verification of identity to the extent that it is reasonable and practical

Question 25

As per the Homeowner's Protection Act, what is not a required disclosure document for an adjustable-rate as opposed to a fixed-rate mortgage as it relates to private mortgage insurance?

(A) Initial amortization schedule
(B) PMI termination date
(C) Written notice of cancelation
(D) Exemptions to the right of cancelation

Question 26

The HUD Home Equity Conversion Mortgage Program is primarily for what function?

(A) Reverse mortgages
(B) Insurance for ARMs
(C) Mortgage Insurance for disaster victims
(D) Assisted living

Question 27

Which of the following mortgage types are 100% government insured?

(A) VA
(B) FHA
(C) USDA
(D) Conventional

Question 28

Which of the following is permitted as a part of a qualified loan?

(A) Short term loans
(B) Negative amortization
(C) Interest-only periods
(D) Balloon payments

Question 29

A loan will be taken out for $85,000. What is the cap on the total amount of points and fees for the loan to be considered qualified?

(A) 3% of the total loan
(B) $3,000
(C) 5% of the total loan
(D) $1,000

Question 30

What is not considered a role played by both Fannie Mae and Freddie Mac?

(A) Act as a link between banks and lenders
(B) Provide liquidity to banks
(C) Sell mortgage-backed securities to investors
(D) Guarantee the timely payment of mortgage bonds

Question 31

For a conventional loan where the down payment is 12% for an investment property, what is the maximum amount of seller paid concessions for the transaction?

(A) 2%
(B) 3%
(C) 6%
(D) 9%

Question 32

What scenario listed below allows for the possibility of prepayment penalties?

(A) A loan with a 35-year term
(B) A higher-priced mortgage loan
(C) A fixed-rate conventional loan
(D) An adjustable-rate FHA loan

Question 33

What is the minimum credit score needed to be able to provide a down payment of less than 10% on an FHA loan?

(A) 500
(B) 550
(C) 580
(D) 620

Question 34

What is the maximum amount of a 401(k) type of retirement account that may be used for the purposes of closing costs and down payments without exemptions?

(A) 40%
(B) 50%
(C) 60%
(D) 90%

Question 35

An FHA loan is to be used for a purchase in an area deemed to be classified as the lowest cost market. In 2019, the FHA ceiling is $726,525 and the floor is $314,827. What is the loan limit for the FHA mortgage in this county?

(A) $314,827
(B) $500,000
(C) 110% of the median sale price
(D) $726,525

Question 36

Which of the following loan types are subject to up-front mortgage insurance premiums?

(A) Conventional loan with 20% down
(B) VA loan with 10% down
(C) Conventional loan with 10% down
(D) FHA loan with 20% down

Question 37

Which of the following is not a factor in the determination of VA required minimum residual income?

(A) Family size
(B) Geographical location
(C) Credit score
(D) Loan amount

Question 38

Which of the following is not often a requirement for a Jumbo loan as opposed to a conforming loan?

(A) Minimum 680 credit score
(B) Debt to income ratio no greater than 30%
(C) Minimum down payment of 10%
(D) Additional financial health documentation

Question 39

Of the loan types shown below, which can be considered as a traditional loan?

(A) Interest-only mortgage
(B) Balloon mortgage loan
(C) Jumbo mortgage loan
(D) Payment option adjustable-rate mortgages

Question 40

For a higher-priced mortgage loan, which of the following property types are exempt from needing to include insurance premiums in escrow?

(A) Condominium
(B) Multi-family property
(C) Vacation home
(D) Investment property

Question 41

If a lender requires a payment shock threshold of 200%, what is the highest total monthly mortgage payment that can be borrowed if the current rent payment is $1250/month?

(A) $1250
(B) $2000
(C) $2500
(D) $2850

Question 42

Which of the following is not a factor when determining an individual's debt to income ratio?

(A) Student loans
(B) Gross income
(C) Net income
(D) Credit card payments

Question 43

A 5/5 Adjustable-rate mortgage is one in which:

(A) Is fixed for 5 years then adjustable for 5
(B) Is adjustable for 5 years then fixed for 5
(C) Is fixed for 5 years and then adjusts once every 5 years
(D) Is fixed for 25 years

Question 44

A balloon loan is most appropriate for which of the following scenarios?

(A) A borrower with a high down payment amount
(B) A borrower who will be moving in 2 years
(C) A borrower with a poor credit score
(D) Purchase of a second property

Question 45

Which of the following is not a typical trait of a borrower who can be classified as subprime?

(A) History of a foreclosure
(B) Debt to income ratio of 40% or more
(C) FICO score below 600
(D) History of bankruptcy

Question 46

Which of the following no-income verification loans are most appropriate for an individual with significant assets but currently no job?

(A) Stated income, stated assets
(B) Stated income, verified assets
(C) No income, verified assets
(D) No income, no assets

Question 47

An 80-15-5 Purchase Money Second Mortgage indicates which of the following?

(A) 15% second mortgage, 5% down payment
(B) 15% down payment, 5% second mortgage
(C) 15% down payment, 5% closing costs
(D) 15% second mortgage, 5% closing costs

Question 48

What Is the required time of notice in days from a creditor for any subsequent interest rate changes after the initial change?

(A) Min 210 Max 240
(B) Min 240 Max 300
(C) Min 100 Max 150
(D) Min 60 Max 120

Question 49

A borrower owns a home valued at $450,000 and owes $300,000. He wishes to obtain a Home Equity Line of Credit. The lender is allowing access up to 90% of equity. What is the maximum amount of the HELOC loan?

(A) $50,000
(B) $75,000
(C) $105,000
(D) $150,000

Question 50

Which of the following Home Equity Conversion Mortgage payment plans require the borrower to live in the home as a primary residence?

(A) Lump-sum
(B) Line of credit
(C) Modified term
(D) Tenure

Question 51

A reverse mortgage has which of the following characteristics in regard to debt and equity for the borrower?

(A) Debt increases and equity increases
(B) Debt decreases and equity increases
(C) Debt increases and equity decreases
(D) Debt decreases and equity decreases

Question 52

Which of the following is false concerning a construction-to-permanent type loan?

(A) Only interest is paid during construction
(B) The interest rate is often variable during construction
(C) The loan requires only a single closing
(D) A maximum mortgage rate cannot be locked in

Question 53

Which of the following loan types can be considered a junior lien?

(A) Home equity loan
(B) Construction loan
(C) Adjustable-rate mortgage
(D) Fixed-rate mortgage

Question 54

If a borrower is delinquent on payments and the bank agrees to allow the borrower to sell the home for less than is owed, they are agreeing to which of the following?

(A) Forbearance
(B) Foreclosure
(C) Short Sale
(D) Extension of payment

Question 55

An early payment default is a loan that is how many days delinquent?

(A) 30
(B) 60
(C) 90
(D) 120

Question 56

A borrower takes out a yield-spread premium loan which includes -2.250 points. Which of the following statements are true?

(A) The borrower receives a rebate of $2250 which can be used towards closing costs
(B) The borrower will owe $2250 at closing
(C) The loan will be $2250 higher than the original amount
(D) The loan will be $2250 lower than the original amount

Question 57

A simple-interest mortgage has a rate of 4.0% and a current balance of $100,000. What is the interest due at the end of a 30-day period?

(A) $225
(B) $329
(C) $380
(D) $425

Question 58

Which of the following types of real estate conveyance is abolished in most states?

(A) Fee tail
(B) Fee simple
(C) Life estate
(D) Defeasible estate

Question 59

A mortgage loan was purchased by Fannie Mae after closing. Payments from the borrower are made through Bank "A," but the loan is financed through Fannie Mae. What role is Bank "A" occupying in this transaction?

(A) Mortgage broker
(B) Mortgage lender
(C) Mortgage investor
(D) Mortgage Servicer

Question 60

Which of the following is a true statement regarding origination fees?

(A) They are a fixed fee for every transaction
(B) They are non-negotiable
(C) They can be substituted for a commission based off of yield spread premium
(D) They are the same regardless of the sale price

Question 61

The 1003 mortgage application loan form requires up to how many years of employment to be recorded for each applicant?

(A) 1
(B) 2
(C) 3
(D) 5

Question 62

Which of the following people is a borrower not eligible to receive a gift from in which to cover costs at closing?

(A) Son
(B) Fiancé
(C) Legal guardian
(D) The real estate agent

Question 63

A credit report will record credit checks from multiple mortgage lenders as a single inquiry for how many days?

(A) 15
(B) 30
(C) 45
(D) 60

Question 64

Which of the following asset types will be reduced when being considered on a mortgage application?

(A) Retirement funds
(B) Savings account
(C) Checking account
(D) Stocks and bonds

Question 65

To receive a verbal verification of employment, a lender may call an employer no more than _____ days before closing according to Fannie Mae requirements?

(A) 10
(B) 15
(C) 30
(D) 45

Question 66

A borrower signs a Certification and Authorization form which allows for all of the following except:

(A) Certification from the borrower that all information is correct and accurate
(B) Ability for the lender to sell the loan to another company
(C) Agreement with the closing disclosure
(D) Release of credit information

Question 67

Which of the following fee tolerance thresholds permit a 0% increase in fees from the loan estimate to the closing disclosure?

(A) Zero tolerance
(B) 10% cumulative tolerance
(C) no or unlimited tolerance
(D) Tiered tolerance

Question 68

If consummation for a loan is to occur on a Monday, which of the following days of the previous week is the latest that the closing disclosure can be provided?

(A) Tuesday
(B) Wednesday
(C) Thursday
(D) Friday

Question 69

If a revised loan estimate is to be provided, it must be received by the borrower no more than how many days in advance of consummation?

(A) 3
(B) 7
(C) 10
(D) 15

Question 70

If a lender denies the application of the borrower on the second day after the application was provided, what is the minimum amount of days in which the special information pamphlet must be provided?

(A) The pamphlet need not be provided
(B) 3
(C) 10
(D) 15

Question 71

Which of the following is not a condition in which if applicable allows for a HUD housing counseling service to include a fee for a pre-purchase?

(A) A person who demonstrates they cannot afford the fee must be provided service without charge
(B) An advance fee structure must be provided
(C) Fees must not exceed 1% of the current loan
(D) Fees must commensurate with the level of service provided

Question 72

A borrower has a 40-hour work week and is paid $22.52 per hour; what is the monthly income?

(A) $3,903.47
(B) $4,222.55
(C) $4,688.66
(D) $5,101.72

Question 73

According to the TILA-RESPA integrated disclosures, all of the following must be included in the loan estimate to consider it received except:

(A) Property sale history
(B) Consumer name
(C) Consumer income
(D) Property address

Question 74

Calculate the required prepaid costs on a loan estimate. The property tax requirement is 3 months at an annual cost of $5000/year. The homeowner's insurance requirement is 6 months at a rate of $1100/year and there are 10 days of interest required at 17.25 per day at a rate of 4.5%.

(A) $1972
(B) $2025
(C) $2200
(D) $2435

Question 75

For the "calculating cash to close" section of the loan estimate, determine the amount to place under "funds for borrower" in a refinance if the total amount of all existing debt being satisfied in the transaction minus the principal amount of debt extended is $500.

(A) $0
(B) $500
(C) -$500
(D) $250

Question 76

A loan amount is $200,000. The total amount of interest that will be paid over the loan term is $100,000. Calculate the Total Interest Percentage (TIP).

(A) 25%
(B) 50%
(C) 75%
(D) 100%

Question 77

Which of the following is a charge for a late payment?

(A) An increase in the interest rate triggered by a late payment
(B) The right of acceleration
(C) Fees imposed for actual collection costs
(D) Referral charges

Question 78

How long after consummation may a revised closing disclosure be provided?

(A) 15 business days
(B) 15 calendar days
(C) 30 calendar days
(D) 30 business days

Question 79

If an escrow account is not established, the estimated property costs must be provided over what time period in the closing disclosure?

(A) 3 months
(B) 6 months
(C) 9 months
(D) 1 year

Question 80

What is not considered satisfactory documentation of an earnest money deposit if required from a lender?

(A) Copy of the borrower's canceled check
(B) Certification from the deposit holder acknowledging receipt of funds
(C) Last two paystubs
(D) Separate evidence of the fund source

Question 81

If an acceptable gift is to be provided at closing in the form of an electric wire transfer from the donor, which of the following is a required documentation for the gift?

(A) Withdrawal statement from the donor account
(B) Bank statement of the donor account
(C) Wire transfer documentation from the donor
(D) Copy of the certified check

Question 82

Which of the following is an acceptable form of sweat equity?

(A) Repairs listed on the appraisal
(B) Cash back for repairs
(C) Delayed work
(D) Debris removal

Question 83

Which of the following is not used in the calculation of a borrower's liabilities?

(A) Revolving charge accounts
(B) Lease payments
(C) Federal taxes
(D) Alimony

Question 84

For capital gains to be considered income, what is the minimum required history?

(A) 6 months
(B) 1 year
(C) 2 years
(D) 5 years

Question 85

Which of the following appraisal types is most appropriate for an entire apartment complex?

(A) Market approach
(B) Income approach
(C) Cost approach
(D) None of the above

Question 86

A title search comes back with an indication that the local railroad company has the ability to access part of the home's land for access to the tracks. This can be classified as which of the following issues resulting from the title search?

(A) Lien
(B) Encumbrance
(C) Easement
(D) Survey dispute

Question 87

During the life of a loan, FEMA has determined that a property that was previously in the moderate-risk flood zone, is now in a high-risk flood zone. Which of the following statements is true regarding the requirements for flood insurance?

(A) FEMA now requires the property to get flood insurance
(B) FEMA allows a 10-year grace period until the property is required to get flood insurance
(C) The property is grandfathered in and does not require flood insurance
(D) FEMA recommends flood insurance, but it is not required

Question 88

How long is the period of the right to rescind after closing for the refinance of a residential property?

(A) 0 days
(B) 3 days
(C) 7 days
(D) 10 days

Question 89

Calculate the per diem interest over a 30-day period if a loan has a balance of $242,000 and an interest rate of 4.25%.

(A) $34.25
(B) $710.22
(C) $744.23
(D) $845.34

Question 90

A proposed loan amount of $300,000 will have an interest rate of 4.25%. However, the borrower chooses to buy 2 points on the loan for a lower interest rate. Considering only the loan amount and the points, what is the new amount to be financed?

(A) $300,600
(B) $306,000
(C) $360,000
(D) $294,000

Question 91

A borrower has an adjustable-rate mortgage with an initial fixed rate of 5.0%. At the time the fixed rate expires, the index is determined to be 3% and the margin is 2.5%. If the outstanding balance on the loan is $158,000, what is the increase in the monthly interest-only for the first month of the adjustable rate?

(A) $65.83
(B) $95.66
(C) $101.22
(D) $145.90

Question 92

A borrower has an existing mortgage principal of $230,000 on a home that is valued at $280,000. The borrower wishes to purchase a second home at a total cost of $220,000. What percent down on the second home must the borrower put to keep the combined LTV at 80%?

(A) 15%
(B) 18%
(C) 20%
(D) 23%

Question 93

What is the front end and back end maximum qualifying FHA debt ratios?

(A) 28/40
(B) 31/43
(C) 35/48
(D) 38/50

Question 94

Which of the following statements is most often true regarding adjustable rate mortgages?

(A) Only the index remains the same
(B) Only the index can change over time
(C) The margin and the index can change over time
(D) The margin and the index remain the same

Question 95

Documentation for a large deposit when verifying a borrower's assets is required if the deposit exceeds what percent of the sale price?

(A) 1%
(B) 2%
(C) 3%
(D) 5%

Question 96

An applicant for a USDA loan has a history of employment that includes 5 years of work history and then 18 months of unemployment. The applicant is now employed again. What is the minimum length of time needed at the new job?

(A) 0 months
(B) 6 months
(C) 1 year
(D) 2 years

Question 97

Which of the following is not one of the three prohibitions as per the Gramm-Leach Bliley Act?

(A) Right to Access
(B) Financial Privacy
(C) Safeguard Rule
(D) Pretexting Prohibition

Question 98

According to RESPA, what is the maximum allowable "cushion" for a borrower's escrow account that a lender can require?

(A) 1/12 of yearly disbursements
(B) 1/6 of yearly disbursements
(C) 1% of the total loan
(D) 3% of the total loan

Question 99

Which of the following is not a red-flag related to the sales contract?

(A) Purchaser is not the applicant
(B) Real estate commission is excessive
(C) Power of attorney used
(D) Recently issued Social Security number

Question 100

Which of the following is an acceptable action when determining if an offer can be classified as "Bona Fide"?

(A) Refusal to sell the advertised product
(B) Trying to sell a different product
(C) Disparagement of the advertised product
(D) Refusal to take orders of the advertised products

Question 101

Which of the following is not exempted from the Fair Housing Act?

(A) Rental of a room in a dwelling with no more than four independent units
(B) Housing operated by private organizations
(C) Housing operated by private clubs
(D) Multi-family home without the use of a broker or real estate agent

Question 102

Which of the following is the most commonly reported complaint related to mortgage lending?

(A) Mortgage servicing
(B) Misapplied funds
(C) Contract errors
(D) Contract filing

Question 103

Which of the following is not an acceptable practice for a mortgage loan officer acting on behalf of the lender?

(A) Gather income information
(B) Prescreen the applicant for approval
(C) Submit the application to the lender
(D) Gather employment information

Question 104

The act of encouraging repeated refinancing of a loan without any real benefit to the borrower is which of the following practices?

(A) Redlining
(B) Steering
(C) Flipping
(D) Ballooning

Question 105

Which of the following fees are not allowed for a VA loan?

(A) Discount points
(B) Attorney fees charged by a lender
(C) Lender fee
(D) Title insurance

Question 106

When a power of attorney is granted for a real estate transaction, which of the following defines the role of the principal?

(A) The person granting authority to someone else
(B) The person gaining authority
(C) The attorney to process the transaction
(D) The agent to process the transaction

Question 107

According to the Equal Credit Opportunity Act, which of the following is not an acceptable reason for the lender to request the credit report of a spouse?

(A) The spouse will be permitted to use the account
(B) The spouse is contractually liable for the account
(C) The applicant is relying on the spouse's income for repayment
(D) The applicant has been married for over 2 years

Question 108

As per the SAFE Mortgage Licensing Act, which of the following is not a state requirement for the system of licensing for residential mortgage loan originators?

(A) Criminal history
(B) Continuing education
(C) Pre-approval
(D) Pre-licensure education

Question 109

The Loan Originator Rule regulates compensation paid to the loan originator in most closed-end transactions which includes all of the following except:

(A) Prohibition of the terms of compensation from being based on the terms of the transaction
(B) Prohibition of compensation due to bonuses related to mortgage activities
(C) Permitting certain compensation methods such as retirement plans based on mortgage-related profits
(D) Prohibition of compensation by a 2nd party

Question 110

CFPB civil penalties are assessed in which of the following ways?

(A) Single lump-sum penalty
(B) Penalty for each infraction
(C) Penalty only for an infraction in which the regulation was knowingly violated
(D) Penalty for each day during which the violation continues

Question 111

What is not a true statement regarding the characteristics of NMLS unique identifiers?

(A) The entity's unique ID can only be changed by request once per year
(B) The numbers are assigned sequentially
(C) Each branch within a company is assigned a unique ID
(D) Each natural person is assigned a unique ID

Question 112

As per SAFE Act requirements, a Mortgage Loan Originator must submit all of the following except:

(A) Fingerprints for background check
(B) Social Security Number
(C) Financial services employment history for the prior ten years
(D) Disclosure and justification of time of unemployment

Question 113

The NMLS Registry has the intended purpose of all of the following except:

(A) Provide licensing database
(B) Enhance consumer protections
(C) Ensure individualized license applications
(D) Facilitate the collection and disbursement of consumer complaints

Question 114

A unique identifier shall be provided to a consumer in all of the following scenarios except:

(A) Through any initial written communication
(B) Before acting as a mortgage loan originator
(C) Upon request
(D) In any finalized documents

Question 115

What is a requirement for a licensed mortgage originator and not a registered mortgage originator?

(A) Submit fingerprints for background check
(B) Submit personal history
(C) Acquire unique identifier
(D) Take 20 hours of pre-license education

Question 116

A property is bought and the appraisal is artificially inflated. The home is resold shortly after purchase at a profit. Which of the following illegal tactics is likely being employed?

(A) Redlining
(B) Flipping
(C) Mortgage fraud
(D) Coercion

Question 117

An individual who performs only which of the actions below cannot be defined as a loan originator as per the Loan Origination Rule?

(A) Clerical tasks on behalf of a loan originator
(B) Takes an application
(C) Arranges a credit transaction
(D) Offers credit terms

Question 118

A lender offers a discount for the "bundling" of settlement services where the consumer can pay a lower price in total for the combination of the services. What statement must be true for the lender to not be in violation of RESPA?

(A) The use of the combination must be optional
(B) The sum of the individual services must equal the combination price
(C) The discount must be made up for in other fees
(D) The discount must not exceed 10%

Question 119

An applicant alters a tax return to indicate a higher yearly income. What type of fraud is being committed?

(A) Material misrepresentation
(B) Material misstatements
(C) Omission
(D) None of the above

Question 120

When determining an applicant's ability to repay for an adjustable-rate mortgage, what rate is used to evaluate?

(A) The fixed-rate
(B) The fully indexed rate
(C) The greater of the fully indexed rate or fixed rate
(D) The lesser of the fully indexed rate or fixed rate

Question 121

Which of the following exempts a mortgage from having a Safe Harbor?

(A) The mortgage is a higher-priced loan
(B) The mortgage is a qualified loan
(C) The mortgage meets ATR requirements
(D) The DTI ratio must be below a minimum threshold

Question 122

What is not a function of the CFPB?

(A) Conduct research on consumer behavior
(B) Investigate consumer complaints
(C) Alert consumers to possible risks
(D) Dictate recommended consumer actions

Question 123

CFPB allows a consumer how long to provide feedback about a company's response?

(A) 15 days
(B) 30 days
(C) 45 days
(D) 60 days

Question 124

The TILA Escrow Rule states that Higher-priced mortgages must maintain an escrow account for a period of:

(A) 1 year
(B) 3 years
(C) 5 years
(D) 10 years

Question 125

As per Regulation V, eligibility information about a consumer from a third party may not be used unless an opt-out option is provided. What is an unreasonable method of obtaining the opt-out?

(A) A consumer letter
(B) Check off box
(C) Including a reply form with a self-addressed envelope
(D) Electronic means of opting-out

Question 126

Which of the following is an example of a violation of "required use" as per RESPA?

(A) Failure to provide required disclosures
(B) A real estate agent requiring the use of a particular loan officer
(C) Failure to provide the required information for an Estimate
(D) Failure to provide a loan estimate

Question 127

A mortgage broker is permitted to charge a fee as a condition for providing an estimate for which of the following as per RESPA?

(A) Appraisal
(B) Inspection
(C) Credit Report
(D) Any settlement services

Question 128

According to RESPA, a Good Faith Estimate expires after how many days without an intent to proceed?

(A) 7
(B) 10
(C) 21
(D) 30

Question 129

As per RESPA, which of the following charges on an estimate are allowed to be within 10% of the actual settlement charges?

(A) Origination charge
(B) Transfer taxes
(C) Lender required settlement charges
(D) The credit or charge for the interest rate

Question 130

As per the ECOA, at what age is someone considered elderly?

(A) 62
(B) 65
(C) 68
(D) 70

Question 131

As per the ECOA, a creditor shall notify an applicant of action taken within _____ days after taking adverse action on an existing account.

(A) 15
(B) 30
(C) 60
(D) 90

Question 132

As per ECOA, a creditor is able to consider the inclusion of a source of income based on which of the following?

(A) Part-time vs full-time income
(B) Income from a pension
(C) Probability of continuance
(D) Income from alimony

Question 133

When a creditor requires a cosigner due to the applicant's creditworthiness, what is an acceptable requirement that may be placed on who is chosen as the other person?

(A) Geographical location
(B) Relationship to client
(C) Age of the other person
(D) Marital status

Question 134

According to the Truth in Lending Act, how many hard copies of a right to rescind must be provided to each consumer if electronic distribution is not available?

(A) 1
(B) 2
(C) 3
(D) 4

Question 135

An advertisement uses the term "fixed" to describe a rate for a non-variable rate transaction where the payment will increase in a stepped fashion. According to the Truth in Lending Act, which of the following must accompany the term "fixed" in the advertisement in close proximity?

(A) The term "Variable Rate Mortgage"
(B) The term "Fixed Rate Mortgage"
(C) The term "ARM"
(D) The time period for which the payment is fixed

Question 136

What is the minimum term in years of a balloon loan that does not qualify as a bridge loan?

(A) 2
(B) 5
(C) 10
(D) 30

Question 137

For a given transaction, the average prime offer rate is determined to be 5.5%. For a first-lien transaction of $50,000 or more, what is the minimum APR that would qualify the transaction as a high-cost mortgage?

(A) 8%
(B) 10%
(C) 11.5%
(D) 12%

Question 138

All of the following are exceptions for a higher-priced mortgage to be required to have an escrow account except:

(A) A transaction secured by shares in a cooperative
(B) A loan of less than 5 years
(C) A transaction to finance the initial construction of a dwelling
(D) A reverse mortgage transaction subject to section 1026.33

Question 139

To avoid prohibited steering, what is not an example of a required loan type that must be presented to the consumer?

(A) The loan with the lowest interest rate
(B) The loan with the lowest interest rate without a prepayment penalty
(C) The loan with the lowest total dollar amount
(D) The loan with the lowest origination fees

Question 140

Which of the following scenarios would not meet the requirements of a dwelling as per the Home Mortgage Disclosure Act?

(A) A mixed-use property which is determined to be 80% commercial
(B) A multifamily residential structure
(C) A condominium
(D) A vacation Home

Question 141

For how long will a chapter 13 bankruptcy remain on a credit report?

(A) 5 years
(B) 7 years
(C) 10 years
(D) 15 years

Question 142

What statement below does not potentially qualify a creditor for the "red flag" rule?

(A) Payment for goods or services is immediate
(B) The creditor grants or arranges credit.
(C) The creditor participates in the decision to set the terms of credit
(D) Information is provided to credit reporting companies in connection with a credit transaction

Question 143

What is not an example of nonpublic information?

(A) Phone number from a telephone book
(B) Social security provided through a financial service
(C) Information obtained through internet cookies
(D) Credit score

Question 144

As per the E-Sign Act, what is not a required disclosure that must be provided from the financial institution to the consumer?

(A) Right to sign paper copies
(B) Describing processes for E-Signature
(C) The right to withdraw
(D) Any fees or conditions associated with withdrawal

Question 145

As per the US Patriot Act, what is not a minimum requirement in regard to concentration accounts for financial institutions?

(A) Clients shall not be allowed to direct transactions with the account
(B) The financial institution shall not inform customers of the existence of the account
(C) The financial institution shall establish written procedures for the documentation of transactions
(D) The financial institution shall limit the number of transactions per day of a concentration account

Question 146

What HUD program provides law enforcement officers, teachers, firefighters, and emergency medical technicians with the opportunity to purchase homes located in revitalization areas at a discount?

(A) Rehabilitation Loan Mortgage Insurance
(B) Assisted Living Conversion Program
(C) Good Neighbor Next Door
(D) Self-Help Housing Property Disposition

Question 147

The Fair Housing Act was enacted to protect against which of the following?

(A) Energy efficiency
(B) Community development
(C) Multifamily requirements
(D) Housing discrimination

Question 148

In which of the following situations is a homeowner not eligible for counseling as per the Homeownership Counseling Act?

(A) The loan is secured by the owner's primary residence
(B) The loan is assisted by the Farmer Home Administration
(C) There is an expectation that the homeowner will be unable to make payments
(D) There is a significant reduction in the household income

Question 149

What type of transaction below is not exempt from the ability to repay rule?

(A) A 12-month construction-to-permanent loan
(B) Reverse mortgages
(C) Time-share plans
(D) Higher-Priced loan

Question 150

For a Quality Mortgage to fall under the temporary definition, it must meet all of the general requirements as well as one of the following except:

(A) Eligible for FHA insurance
(B) Eligible to be guaranteed by the VA
(C) Eligible to be guaranteed by the USDA
(D) Eligible for USDA insurance

Question 151

What is the maximum amount of seller concessions for an FHA loan?

(A) 2%
(B) 3%
(C) 6%
(D) 10%

Question 152

What type of loan is subject to Loan Level Price adjustments?

(A) Conventional
(B) FHA
(C) USDA
(D) VA

Question 153

Which of the following uses a Desktop Underwriter for the purposes of Automated Underwriting Systems?

(A) Fannie Mae
(B) Freddie Mac
(C) VA
(D) USDA

Question 154

Which of the following types of loans is it acceptable to have a 0% down payment?

(A) Conventional
(B) VA
(C) FHA
(D) None of the above

Question 155

What is not an acceptable condition of property hazard insurance as per the requirements by Fannie Mae?

(A) Coverage against fire, wind, rain, and other hazards
(B) Claims to be settled on an Actual Value Basis
(C) Inclusion of a separate policy to meet requirements
(D) An endorsement by a second company to satisfy requirements

Question 156

What is the maximum amount of a prepayment penalty for the first two years of the life of a loan?

(A) 1%
(B) 2%
(C) 3%
(D) 5%

Question 157

A national guard member with a down payment of 5% for a first-time use is required to pay what amount for the VA Funding Fee?

(A) 1.25%
(B) 1.5%
(C) 1.75%
(D) 2.4%

Question 158

A VA applicant has $6000 in monthly income. If they have a $1200 mortgage, $400 in revolving debt, and $200 in utilities. What is the estimated monthly residual income?

(A) $4200
(B) $4400
(C) $4800
(D) $5800

Question 159

At what loan-to-value percentage will PMI be automatically removed on a conventional loan?

(A) 75%
(B) 78%
(C) 80%
(D) 90%

Question 160

Which of the following is an accurate statement as it relates to the characteristics of a jumbo loan?

(A) A jumbo loan is not government-backed
(B) A jumbo loan must use a fixed rate
(C) A jumbo loan must use an adjustable-rate
(D) The loan amount is capped by federal conforming loan limits

Question 161

Which of the following is not a scenario where payment shock is considered?

(A) First time home buyers
(B) Adjustable-rate mortgages
(C) Transition from rental to purchase
(D) Fixed-rate mortgages

Question 162

A borrower must keep his debt-to-income ratio at 40% maximum. She has $500 and $300 per month in credit card payments and student loans respectively. What is the maximum allowable monthly total mortgage payment if her monthly gross income is $5750?

(A) $1200
(B) $1500
(C) $2000
(D) $2200

Question 163

A 5/1 adjustable-rate mortgage has a margin of 2%. At the end of year 6, the index is determined to be 4%. What is the mortgage rate for year 7?

(A) 4%
(B) 5%
(C) 6%
(D) 7%

Question 164

What is not a common index used for the determinization of the index rate for ARMs?

(A) Maturity yield on one-year Treasury Bills
(B) 11th District cost of funds index
(C) London Interbank Offered rate
(D) Consumer Price Index

Question 165

Which of the following no-income verification loans are most appropriate for a small business owner which keeps all assets in a business account and does not distribute pay stubs?

(A) Stated income, stated assets
(B) Stated income, verified assets
(C) No income, verified assets
(D) No income, no assets

Question 166

Which of the following scenarios is most likely suited for a non-qualified loan?

(A) Self-employed for ten years with documented income
(B) Very High DTI but substantial reserves
(C) Credit score below 550
(D) Loans with 10-year terms

Question 167

The primary purpose of a purchase money second mortgage is which of the following?

(A) Reduce or eliminate the need for a down payment
(B) Obtain a loan with a low credit score
(C) Decrease the monthly mortgage payment
(D) Decrease the term of the loan

Question 168

For a conventional fixed-rate mortgage loan, which of the following may cause a variation in the borrower's total home monthly payment?

(A) Interest payment
(B) Principal payment
(C) Property taxes
(D) Interest rate

Question 169

A borrower with a 5/1 adjustable-rate mortgage has an initial fixed rate of 5% with a margin of 2%. The lifetime adjustment cap is 4% and the periodic adjustment cap is 1.5%. The index for year seven is 4% and the index for year eight is 6%. What is the rate for year eight?

(A) 6%
(B) 6.5%
(C) 7.5%
(D) 8.0%

Question 170

What is the required time of notice in days from a creditor for a first-time interest rate change?

(A) Min 210 Max 240
(B) Min 240 Max 300
(C) Min 100 Max 150
(D) Min 30 Max 90

Question 171

Which of the following is not a commonality between a Home Equity Line of Credit (HELOC) and a Home Equity Loan?

(A) Use of home equity
(B) Property is used as collateral
(C) Usually uses a fixed rate
(D) Shorter terms than traditional mortgages

Question 172

In general, what is the minimum amount of equity required to be considered for a reverse mortgage?

(A) 50%
(B) 60%
(C) 75%
(D) 100%

Question 173

Which of the following loan types require two sets of fees to be applied at closing?

(A) Construction-to-permanent loan
(B) Jumbo loan
(C) Balloon loan
(D) Construction only loan

Question 174

A borrower is more than 90 days late on payments and has received a notice of default from the lender, but no action has been taken to this point. At what state is the property in?

(A) Escrow default
(B) Short sale
(C) Pre-foreclosure
(D) Foreclosure

Question 175

If a yield spread premium is used, how must it be disclosed?

(A) On the HUD-1 form
(B) In a letter from the lender at closing
(C) At the time of rate lock
(D) On the closing disclosure

Question 176

What is the maximum reduction in the interest rate for the first year of a 2-1 buydown mortgage?

(A) 0.5%
(B) 1.0%
(C) 1.5%
(D) 2.0%

Question 177

If a borrower chooses to execute a cash-out refinance which of the following statements are true?

(A) There are no fees associated
(B) The final amount owed is greater than the original
(C) The final amount owed is less than the original
(D) Equity increases after the transaction are complete

Question 178

Which of the following types of conveyance is characterized by providing absolute ownership of a property?

(A) Fee tail
(B) Fee simple
(C) Life estate
(D) Defeasible estate

Question 179

Which of the following third-party provider types can view specific information from your account after consent is provided?

(A) Payment Initiation Service Provider (PISP)
(B) Account Information Service Provider (AISP)
(C) Third-Party Payment Plan
(D) Third-Party Transaction

Question 180

Which of the following entities cannot be considered a part of the primary mortgage market?

(A) Mortgage bankers
(B) Mortgage brokers
(C) Credit unions
(D) Mortgage aggregator

Question 181

If a borrower takes on an assumable mortgage from a lender, which of the following statements are true in regard to the effect on the existing interest rate?

(A) The rate remains the same
(B) The rate increases despite the market
(C) The rate will change based on the market
(D) The rate will decrease

Question 182

A borrower is to receive a gift of funds to cover closing costs for a one-unit primary residence. The anticipated LTV is 70%. What is the minimum borrower contribution requirement from their own funds as per Fannie Mae requirements?

(A) 0%
(B) 3%
(C) 5%
(D) 10%

Question 183

For funds to be considered "seasoned", an applicant must be able to produce documents showing that the funds have been in the account for how many days?

(A) 60
(B) 90
(C) 120
(D) 180

Question 184

Which of the following is most often used to verify the income of a self-employed mortgage applicant?

(A) Bank statements
(B) Savings account
(C) Assets
(D) Tax return

Question 185

A mortgage applicant is provided with a loan estimate which includes $5000 in recording fees and is subject to the 10% cumulative fee limit. What is the maximum amount for the recording fees that are acceptable on the closing disclosure?

(A) $5000
(B) $5200
(C) $5450
(D) $5500

Question 186

If a recording fee decreases from the loan estimate to the closing disclosure, which of the following statements are true?

(A) The fee is not included in the cumulation of fees
(B) The fee is included in the cumulation of fees
(C) The fee is not included in the cumulation of fees for the zero-tolerance requirement
(D) The fee is included in the cumulation of fees for the zero-tolerance requirement only

Question 187

How many business days after the receipt of a loan application must the initial loan estimate be provided?

(A) 3
(B) 7
(C) 10
(D) 30

Question 188

All of the following fees must appear on the loan estimate regardless of if they are applicable to the loan except:

(A) Points
(B) Recording fees and other taxes
(C) Inspection fee
(D) Transfer taxes

Question 189

If the consumer does not provide an intent to proceed, how long does it take in days for the initial loan estimate to expire?

(A) 10
(B) 15
(C) 21
(D) 30

Question 190

A valid change in circumstance includes all of the following except:

(A) Substantial increase in assets of the consumer
(B) Requested revision to the credit terms
(C) The interest rate was not locked
(D) Intent to proceed was provided after the expiration date

Question 191

A revised closing disclosure is issued and it includes an interest rate that has changed from fixed to variable. What is the correct course of action?

(A) The closing can proceed as scheduled
(B) The change should trigger a 3-day waiting period
(C) The change should trigger a 10-day waiting period
(D) The change requires a revised loan estimate

Question 192

The special information booklet need not be provided for all of the following except:

(A) Refinance
(B) Reverse mortgage
(C) Variable-rate loans
(D) Closed-end loans

Question 193

A third-party service charge is not subject to the 10% cumulative tolerance in which of the following scenarios?

(A) The charge is not paid to the creditor
(B) The charge is not paid to the creditor's affiliate
(C) The consumer chose a third party on a written list of service providers by the creditor
(D) The consumer chose a third party not on a written list of service providers by the creditor

Question 194

Which of the following is not an option for finding a HUD approved counselor?

(A) CFPB find a counselor tool
(B) Call HOPE 24/7 hotline
(C) Call HUD Hotline
(D) Call CFPB

Question 195

Values in a closing disclosure are rounded to:

(A) The nearest cent
(B) The nearest 10 cents
(C) The nearest dollar
(D) The nearest 10 dollar

Question 196

Which of the following items is appropriate to be included in the "Other" section of the closing disclosure?

(A) Mortgage insurance premium
(B) Home warranties
(C) Prepaid interest
(D) Property taxes

Question 197

Which of the following documents is not required to be provided for the purchase of a primary residence?

(A) Loan estimate
(B) Closing disclosure
(C) Notice of the right to rescind
(D) Initial escrow statement

Question 198

Which of the following holidays can still be considered a business day?

(A) Veterans Day
(B) The Friday after Thanksgiving
(C) Columbus Day
(D) Labor Day

Question 199

On a loan estimate, a borrower has total closing costs of $8200. The down payment will be $19,500. If a deposit of $5000 was provided previously, calculate the estimated cash to close.

(A) $11300
(B) $19500
(C) $22700
(D) $27700

Question 200

The lender must verify the earnest money deposit if the amount exceeds what percent of the sales price?

(A) 1%
(B) 2%
(C) 3%
(D) 5%

Question 201

Which of the following limits is placed on Social Security as qualifying income?

(A) Social Security must be likely to continue beyond 3 years
(B) Supplemental Security Income (SSI) is not applicable
(C) Only 50% of Social security income qualifies for a loan
(D) Verification is not needed

Question 202

An applicant for an FHA loan has a history of employment that includes 5 years of work history and then 18 months of unemployment. The applicant is now employed again. What is the minimum length of time needed at the new job?

(A) 3 months
(B) 6 months
(C) 1 year
(D) 2 years

Question 203

Which of the following is not a main factor to consider when a credit score is determined?

(A) Income
(B) Credit utilization
(C) Payment history
(D) Length of credit

Question 204

A mortgage applicant has a yearly salary of $60,000/year. The home he wishes to purchase has a monthly tax bill of $450/month, insurance of $90/month, and PMI of $120/month. What is the maximum mortgage amount to keep the housing ratio to 28% or less?

(A) $740
(B) $890
(C) $1100
(D) $1350

Question 205

Which of the following appraisal types is most appropriate for a school building?

(A) Market approach
(B) Income approach
(C) Cost approach
(D) None of the above

Question 206

As per ECOA, an applicant must be informed of the right to receive an appraisal within _____ business days of the receipt of the application.

(A) 3
(B) 7
(C) 10
(D) 30

Question 207

Which of the following is not considered a valid valuation as determined by ECOA?

(A) An appraiser's report
(B) A report by a government-sponsored entity
(C) A broker opinion price
(D) Any publicly available valuation

Question 208

Which of the following is not a violation of ensuring appraiser independence?

(A) Encouraging a targeted value
(B) Withholding appraiser payment
(C) Providing further detail for consideration
(D) Mischaracterization of the property

Question 209

Each of the options listed below indicates a characteristic of a different comparable property for a market appraisal, which is most likely to be omitted?

(A) Distance of 0.5 miles
(B) 200 square feet larger
(C) 35 years younger construction
(D) Sold 4 months ago

Question 210

What is a true statement regarding a purchaser's ability to obtain a title report?

(A) The title report must be obtained from a lender recommended title company
(B) The title report must be obtained through an independent title company
(C) The title report must be obtained by the purchaser personally
(D) The title report may be obtained by the purchaser or through a title company

Question 211

As per FEMA flood insurance requirements, the amount of coverage must be the lesser of all of the following except:

(A) The maximum amount of NFIP coverage available for the particular property type
(B) The appraised value of the property
(C) The outstanding principal balance of the loan
(D) The insurable value of the structure

Question 212

A borrower allows the hazard insurance on the property to lapse. If the lender places insurance on the property without the consent of the borrower, it is called which of the following?

(A) Premium insurance
(B) Title insurance
(C) Force-placed insurance
(D) Mortgage insurance

Question 213

Which of the following is a true statement regarding the function of Private Mortgage Insurance?

(A) PMI protects the lender in case of borrower failure to pay
(B) PMI protects the lender and borrower in case of borrower failure to pay
(C) PMI protects the borrower in case of borrower failure to pay
(D) PMI supplements hazard insurance in case of damage

Question 214

A borrower wishes to refinance an existing loan to remove the PMI from the monthly payment. How long after the first payment must she wait to be able to eliminate PMI?

(A) 1 year
(B) 2 years
(C) 5 years
(D) 10 years

Question 215

How long is the period of the right to rescind after closing for the purchase of a residential property?

(A) 0 days
(B) 3 days
(C) 7 days
(D) 10 days

Question 216

For a refinance, the right to rescission period does not begin until all of the following are satisfied except:

(A) The promissory note is signed
(B) Notice of payoff of the original mortgage
(C) Truth in lending disclosure is received
(D) Two copies of the notice of the right to rescind are received

Question 217

A proposed loan amount of $300,000 will have an interest rate of 4.25%. However, the borrower chooses to buy 2 points on the loan for a lower interest rate. What is the new interest rate?

(A) 3.75%
(B) 4.00%
(C) 4.50%
(D) 4.75%

Question 218

A fixed-rate mortgage has a P & I monthly payment of $820. The yearly tax bill is $6000 and the Hazard Insurance is $1200 per year. If the loan includes a PMI of $82 per month, what is the total monthly payment of the loan?

(A) $1288
(B) $1502
(C) $1625
(D) $1822

Question 219

A borrower wishes to refinance a loan after 5 years of payments. The existing loan has an amount of $340,000. The refinance has closing costs of $4000 which will be rolled into the loan. What is the minimum appraisal value of the home in which PMI will no longer be required?

(A) $420,000
(B) $430,000
(C) $440,000
(D) $448,000

Question 220

As per Fannie Mae requirements, what is the maximum DTI which can be approved independent of the eligibility matrix?

(A) 36%
(B) 38%
(C) 42%
(D) 45%

Question 221

As per the Gramm-Leach Bliley Act, what is not a minimum requirement for a disclosure notice on the sharing of non-public information?

(A) How the information is used by affiliates
(B) With whom the information is shared
(C) Safeguards for the information
(D) What information is collected

Question 222

Which of the following was enacted to prevent redlining?

(A) Bank Secrecy Act
(B) Truth in Lending Act
(C) Community Reinvestment Act
(D) US Patriot Act

Question 223

Which of the following roles is responsible for the verification of the loan application?

(A) Mortgage broker
(B) Loan officer
(C) Loan processor
(D) Real estate agent

Question 224

According to Fannie Mae, which of the following would be classified as a High-level Red Flag?

(A) Address discrepancies throughout the file
(B) Unsigned section
(C) Thin credit files
(D) Generic job title

Question 225

Occupancy fraud is committed when which of the following occurs?

(A) The applicant lies about the property being occupied by anyone
(B) The applicant lies about the property being owner-occupied
(C) The applicant occupies an investment property as a principal residence
(D) The applicant occupies the property and rents out a portion of the home

Question 226

A mortgage lender that advertises a low-interest rate that is unattainable and instead tries to sell products in which are costlier is performing which of the following techniques?

(A) Bandwagon advertising
(B) Steering
(C) Bait and switch
(D) Shock advertising

Question 227

The Fair Housing Act requires all of the following to be provided in advertising except:

(A) Include a sentence explanation of the Fair Housing Act in all advertisements
(B) Include the "equal housing lender" slogan in any broadcast advertisement
(C) Display and Equal Housing Opportunity poster wherever mortgage loans are made
(D) Display the Equal Housing Opportunity Logo on all printed promotional material

Question 228

A real estate agent encourages a borrower to lie about their income so that they may be able to afford a more expensive home leading to a higher fee for the transaction. This can be classified as which of the following?

(A) Predatory lending
(B) Steering
(C) Bait and switch
(D) Redlining

Question 229

Which of the following is the practice of channeling prospective buyers to specific neighborhoods based on race, religion, or ethnicity?

(A) Steering
(B) Blockbusting
(C) Redlining
(D) Predatory lending

Question 230

What is not an application type in which the provisions of HMDA apply?

(A) Residential home purchase
(B) Purchase of vacant lot for construction
(C) Residential refinance
(D) Home improvement loan

Question 231

Which tier of penalties includes the person knowingly violating Federal consumer financial law?

(A) First
(B) Second
(C) Third
(D) Fourth

Question 232

Annual license renewal requirements include how many hours of continuing education?

(A) 4
(B) 8
(C) 15
(D) 20

Question 233

If a mortgage loan originator applicant has been convicted of a felony that is not related to fraud, dishonesty, a breach of trust, or money laundering, what is the minimum amount of time that must have passed for the application to be accepted?

(A) Never
(B) 5 years
(C) 7 years
(D) 15 years

Question 234

As per the SAFE Act, a person is considered to be engaging in the business of a loan originator if the individual performs any of the following except:

(A) Takes a residential loan application
(B) Advertises the taking of residential mortgages
(C) Negotiates terms of residential mortgages for compensation
(D) Provides pre-approval services

Question 235

As per the SAFE Act, a mortgage loan officer may make books, papers, records, or any other data available for review to a supervisor for which reason?

(A) At any time requested
(B) Only after a written request
(C) Only after consent is given by the MLO
(D) Records are confidential except as per subpoena

Question 236

In the event of noncompliance with SAFE Act policies, a public comment period of no more than how many days will follow the initial determination?

(A) 10
(B) 15
(C) 30
(D) 60

Question 237

If a licensed MLO leaves the industry, how long until the individual's license expires?

(A) 2 years
(B) 5 years
(C) 7 years
(D) 10 years

Question 238

Any person who violates section 8 of RESPA is subject to which of the following fines?

(A) Up to one year in prison
(B) Up to five years imprisonment
(C) $100,000 fine
(D) $1,000,000 fine

Question 239

Intentional misrepresentation or concealment of material fact defines which of the following types of fraud?

(A) Actual fraud
(B) Constructive fraud
(C) Material misrepresentation
(D) Material misstatements

Question 240

What is not a prohibited practice related to obtaining an appraisal?

(A) Implying future work based on the valuation
(B) Indicating a minimum required valuation for a loan to be approved
(C) A consumer obtaining multiple appraisals
(D) Excluding payment is a valuation that did not meet expectations

Question 241

To prevent illegal flipping, FHA requires purchasers to own a home for how long before selling again?

(A) 3 months
(B) 6 months
(C) 1 year
(D) 2 years

Question 242

As per the ECOA, the applicant is not required to submit which of the following forms of income?

(A) Reliable alimony
(B) Part-time jobs
(C) Public assistance income
(D) Social Security income

Question 243

What is not one of the eight factors that must be considered for the consumer's ability to repay a loan?

(A) Current income
(B) Current employment status
(C) Monthly mortgage payment
(D) Housing history

Question 244

Under the protection of a rebuttable presumption, which statement is true?

(A) Rebuttable presumption provides a higher level of protection than Safe Harbor
(B) If a court determines that the loan is a higher-priced QM the consumer cannot argue
(C) Rebuttable presumption applies to all Qualified Mortgages
(D) Rebuttable presumption provides more legal protection than general ATR requirements but less than Safe Harbor

Question 245

What information is not published when a CFPB complaint is filed?

(A) Date of complaint
(B) Subject of complaint
(C) Description with consent
(D) Incurred penalty

Question 246

As per regulation V, a continuing relation can include any of the following transactions except:

(A) An investment account
(B) loan in which servicing rights are performed
(C) Lease of personal property
(D) Sale of travel insurance

Question 247

A financial institution must establish an identity theft program which has all of the following elements except:

(A) Identify red flags
(B) Provide products to the consumer concerning potential threats
(C) Response to any red flags
(D) Continuous program updates

Question 248

A VA cash-out loan has a maximum loan to value of what?

(A) 70%
(B) 80%
(C) 90%
(D) 100%

Question 249

What statement below is true regarding discount points on adjustable-rate mortgages?

(A) The points apply to the initial rate only
(B) The points apply to the period of the adjustable-rate only
(C) The points apply to both the initial rate and the period of the adjustable rate
(D) Points are not allowed on adjustable-rate mortgages

Question 250

What is not most likely included in the calculation of the APR?

(A) Interest rate
(B) Discount points
(C) Appraisal fee
(D) Underwriting fee

Solution 1

The RESPA includes a section for definitions 1024.2 which states:

"Mortgage broker means a person (other than an employee of a lender) that renders origination services and serves as an intermediary between a borrower and a lender in a transaction involving a federally related mortgage loan, including such a person that closes the loan in its own name in a table funded transaction."

It is important to note that the broker is not an employee of the lender.

The answer is **(C)**

Solution 2

Section 1024.14 covers prohibited actions related to kickbacks or unearned fees. There should be no agreements of an exchange of items of value or referrals as it relates to the execution of the contract. Section (c) indicates that the only permittable situation for the splitting of charges is for actual services.

The answer is **(A)**

Solution 3

At the time of application, the borrower must be provided with the following:

- Special Information Booklet which outlines various settlement services
- Estimate of settlement costs. This is an estimate of charges the borrower is likely to pay at closing
- Mortgage Servicing Disclosure Statement. This indicates the lender's intention to move forward

The Initial Escrow Statement is a breakdown of the estimated escrow payments to be provided by the borrower monthly and is provided later in the process.

The answer is **(C)**

Solution 4

RESPA is concerned with settlement services. Home improvement contractors typically will be involved after the closing occurs, and therefore the requirements do not apply.

The answer is **(C)**

Solution 5

Section 1024.15 covers affiliated business arrangements. The affiliated business disclosure statement covers the nature of the relationship between the person and the referred party. It is indicated that a statement must be provided no later than the time of each referral.

The answer is **(A)**

Solution 6

The ECOA restricts the situations in which the creditor can inquire about the applicant's relationship with a spouse. As per section 1002.5(c), they are:

"1. The spouse will be permitted to use the account;

2. The spouse will be contractually liable on the account;

3. The applicant is relying on the spouse's income as a basis for repayment of the credit requested;

4. The applicant resides in a community property state or is relying on property located in such a state as a basis for repayment of the credit requested; or

5. The applicant is relying on alimony, child support, or separate maintenance payments from a spouse or former spouse as a basis for repayment of the credit requested."

Item five indicates if the applicant is relying on alimony but not if the roles are reversed.

The answer is **(D)**

Solution 7

ECOA provides a clear definition of what falls under the term adverse action in section 1002.2(a) change in the terms of an account does not fall under this definition.

The answer is **(B)**

Solution 8

Denial of an application must accompany a description of the principal reason for denial. The creditor does not have to be specific as to the number of reasons or how or why a factor affected the application, just what the reason was.

The answer is **(B)**

Solution 9

TILA section 1026.15(b) provides the required disclosures to the consumer for a right to rescind. They are as follows:

"1. The retention or acquisition of a security interest in the consumer's principal dwelling.

2. The consumer's right to rescind.

3. How to exercise the right to rescind

4. The effects of rescission.

5. The date the rescission period expires."

In no way should there be a recommendation with the required information.

The answer is **(C)**

Solution 10

Triggering terms are those that if used, will activate additional requirements and specifically those in TILA section 1026.24(d)(2). The triggering terms can be found in section 1026.24(d) and include:

"1. The amount or percentage of any down payment.

2. The number of payments or period of repayment.

3. The amount of any payment.

4. The amount of any finance charge."

The rate of a finance charge does not trigger the additional requirements.

The answer is **(A)**

Solution 11

TILA section 1026.43(d)(ii) covers the standard mortgage definition. The loan term can be up to 40 years, but the rate must be fixed for a minimum of 5 years.

The answer is **(B)**

Solution 12

TILA section 1026.22(a)(ii)(4) indicates that a rate may be considered accurate if it does not vary by more than 1/8 of 1%.

The answer is **(B)**

Solution 13

The Home Ownership and Equity Protection Act covers four types of transactions:

- Purchase-money mortgages
- Refinances
- Closed-end home equity loan
- Open-end credit plans

Reverse mortgages do not fall under HOEPA

The answer is **(D)**

Solution 14

Balloon payments are not generally allowed for high-cost mortgages and are only allowed under three circumstances:

- The payment schedule is adjusted for seasonal or irregular payments
- The loan is a short-term bridge loan
- The creditor meets the criteria for serving a rural or underserved area

Any other scenarios are not allowed.

The answer is **(D)**

Solution 15

TILA section 1026.32 provides the requirements for high-cost mortgages. When the loan exceeds $20,000, the criteria for total points and fees are 5% of the total loan amount.

The answer is **(B)**

Solution 16

TILA Section 1026.35(a) covers the definition of a higher-priced mortgage loan. Section (iii) indicates that for subordinate lien the APR must exceed the APOR by 3.5% or more.

The answer is **(D)**

Solution 17

Section 1003.3 covers exemptions from the need to report. Section (c)(2) indicates that unimproved land need not be reported.

The answer is **(B)**

Solution 18

As per FCRA, fraud alerts are able to be reported by the consumer directly or an individual acting in good faith that has reason to believe fraud has been committed.

The answer is **(C)**

Solution 19

Section 604 covers permissible furnishing of credit reports. Someone taking legal action against a consumer cannot pull credit without consent or court order.

The answer is **(C)**

Solution 20

Suspicious activity reports are not required for an identified suspect of a violation worth $5,000 or less.

The answer is **(B)**

Solution 21

The ability to opt-out must be provided along with a reasonable time frame but the third party for which information will be provided does not have to be identified.

The answer is **(C)**

Solution 22

Calls can be made no later than 9 pm.

The answer is **(C)**

Solution 23

As per section 1014.5, records are required to be kept a minimum of 24 months.

The answer is **(D)**

Solution 24

The Patriot Act at a minimum requires a financial institution to comply with three procedures in regard to identity verification. As per section 326, they are:

- Verify a consumer's identity to a reasonable extent
- Maintain records used for identity verification

- Consult known lists of terrorists and criminals when evaluating any applicant

There is no requirement on the number of specific forms of identification

The answer is **(C)**

Solution 25

By the nature of the adjustable-rate mortgage, an amortization schedule is not required. This is provided in Section 4903 of The Homeowner's Protection Act.

The answer is **(A)**

Solution 26

The Home Equity Conversion Mortgage Program is for elderly people seeking a reverse mortgage.

The answer is **(A)**

Solution 27

The FHA loan is the only which is 100% backed. The VA and USDA are partially and conventional is 0%.

The answer is **(B)**

Solution 28

A qualified loan is less risky and therefore more stable so it does not include aspects that may increase the risk of default. Some of the features which are not permitted are:

- Balloon payments
- Negative amortization
- Interest-only periods
- Loans with terms longer than 30 years

The answer is **(A)**

Solution 29

A qualified loan must meet the cap of the amount of points and fees based on the amount of the loan. It can be determined as follows:

- 3 percent of the total loan amount for a loan greater than or equal to $100,000
- $3,000 for a loan greater than or equal to $60,000 but less than $100,000
- 5 percent of the total loan amount for a loan greater than or equal to $20,000 but less than $60,000
- $1,000 for a loan greater than or equal to $12,500 but less than $20,000
- 8 percent of the total loan amount for a loan less than $12,500

Since the loan amount is $85,000 it is capped at $3,000

The answer is **(B)**

Solution 30

Fannie Mae and Freddie Mac are government entities that purchase most of the home loans in the US and provide liquidity as needed. Part of this is selling mortgage-backed securities. The sister company, Ginnie Mae, is the entity responsible for payments of mortgage bonds and does not fall under Fannie Mae and Freddie Mac's responsibilities.

The answer is **(D)**

Solution 31

For a principal residence or secondary home purchase, the limit on seller concessions is limited depending on the amount of the down payment. However, for an investment property, the down payment does not matter and is a consistent 2%.

The answer is **(A)**

Solution 32

For prepayment penalties to be allowed, all of the following must be true:

- The APR must remain constant
- The loan is qualified
- The loan is not higher-priced

The fixed-rate conventional fits all of the scenarios.

The answer is **(C)**

Solution 33

An FHA loan has a minimum down payment of 3.5% but the credit score of the individual must be at least 580. If it drops to between 500 and 580, the minimum is 10%.

The answer is **(C)**

Solution 34

As per HUD requirements, a maximum of 60% of a retirement account can be used for closing costs or down payments

The answer is **(C)**

Solution 35

FHA sets limits on the amount that can be borrowed. It is dependent on the geographical area in which the loan is taken and the median sale price in that area. However, it can never be higher than the ceiling or lower than the floor in any area. If the county is determined to be in the lowest cost market, this means that the floor will apply.

The answer is **(A)**

Solution 36

The up-front mortgage insurance premium is a closing cost specific to an FHA loan and cannot be avoided regardless of the down payment amount.

The answer is **(D)**

Solution 37

VA residual income is a measure of the amount of income left over monthly after the mortgage and expenses. The minimum is then a function of the size of the family, the geographical location, and whether or not the loan is above or below $80,000. A credit score is not used to determine the minimum residual income.

The answer is **(C)**

Solution 38

Jumbo loans due to being riskier in nature will have more strict requirements than conforming. This includes higher down payments, more documentation, a higher credit score, and some other factors. While some of the numbers presented in this example can vary, a debt to income ratio of 30% is not often enforced. It will typically be much higher such as 45%.

The answer is **(B)**

Solution 39

Non-traditional loans are those which do not adhere to a standard amortization schedule. For instance, an interest-only loan requires payments which do not include any payment of principal. A jumbo loan, while non-conforming, can be a traditional loan.

The answer is **(C)**

Solution 40

Section 1026.35(b)(2)(ii) includes exceptions to the need for escrow on higher-priced mortgage loans. Insurance does not need to be included for properties in which there is a governing association with an obligation to dwelling owners of which condos fall under.

The answer is **(A)**

Solution 41

Payment shock is a concern that lenders may have when an individual has a dramatic increase in monthly obligations. The threshold can be set by a certain percentage or a function of the debt-to-income ratio. In this case with the threshold at 200%, the threshold will be 2 x 1250 = $2500.

The answer is **(C)**

Solution 42

Debt to income is a measure of the monthly debt obligations to the gross income, not the net pay.

The answer is **(C)**

Solution 43

Adjustable-rate mortgages are often denoted by two numbers, the first being the fixed period and the second being the timeframe in which the rate is adjusted. In this case, the loan is fixed for the first five years and then will adjust every 5 years thereafter.

The answer is **(C)**

Solution 44

A balloon payment does not fully amortize over the life of the loan and there is a remaining balance at the end of the term. The advantage can be that the monthly payments and the rates are less. This lends itself to be advantageous in the short term and not the long term. Therefore, if someone were to be sure they are selling in a short period of time, the balloon mortgage may make sense.

The answer is **(B)**

Solution 45

Subprime mortgages are less qualified borrowers. A DTI of 40% while not great is not considered an issue usually. More often it will be closer to or above 50%.

The answer is **(B)**

Solution 46

No-income verification loans provide means for borrowing without proof of income or assets or both. In this case, the lender can verify assets but not income.

The answer is **(C)**

Solution 47

A Purchase money second mortgage is denoted by the percentages made up by each aspect of the loan in the format: First Mortgage-Second Mortgage-Down Payment.

The answer is **(A)**

Solution 48

The creditor must provide notification of a rate change a minimum of 210 days and no more than 240 days for the first notice. Any subsequent changes are 60 days minimum and no more than 120

The answer is **(D)**

Solution 49

The HELOC is a way for a borrower to tap into the equity of an existing home loan for other purposes. To calculate, the borrower is only allowed to have a total owed amount of 90% of the value of the home: 0.90 X 450,000 = $405,000. Then subtract what is already owed: 405,000 – 300,000 = $105,000

The answer is **(C)**

Solution 50

An HECM has a number of options. The tenure payment plan provides a fixed monthly payment as long as the home remains the primary residence. This is also true for the modified tenure option.

The answer is **(D)**

Solution 51

A reverse mortgage provides payment from a lender to a borrower that taps into the existing equity of a home. The equity is reduced as the payments are made. The lender is not buying the home however and the borrower is indeed still responsible for the increase in debt that results from the payments. This is often settled by the selling of the home at completion.

The answer is **(C)**

Solution 52

There are two types of loans for construction: construction-to-permanent loans and stand-alone construction loans. The construction-to-permanent is a single loan comprised of two parts. Therefore, there is only one closing and terms can be set on the mortgage after construction such as a maximum rate. The payments made during construction are interest only.

The answer is **(D)**

Solution 53

A junior lien is a second loan that uses the home as collateral while the original loan is still in place. A home equity loan taps into the value of a home while the existing mortgage still exists.

The answer is **(A)**

Solution 54

If a borrower is delinquent there is a number of actions which can be taken by the lender. A short sale is when the lender agrees to sell the home for less than what is owed.

The answer is **(C)**

Solution 55

Early Payment default is a failure to pay three consecutive payments and is 90 days delinquent.

The answer is **(C)**

Solution 56

A yield-spread premium loan includes negative points. These are the opposite of buying points for a lower interest rate. The borrower actually receives this amount and can use it for closing costs, but the rate will likely be higher.

The answer is **(A)**

Solution 57

A simple-interest loan calculates interest on a daily basis as opposed to monthly like a traditional loan. To calculate, divide the rate by 365 days and multiply by the outstanding balance and then multiply by the number of days in the period:

$$Interest = \left(\frac{0.04}{365}\right)(100{,}000)(30) = \$328.77$$

The answer is **(B)**

Solution 58

A fee tail is a conveyance that restricts the further sale or transfer of the property but is no longer allowed in most of the United States.

The answer is **(A)**

Solution 59

Many loans are purchased by Fannie Mae and Freddie Mac and they finance the loan. A borrower will not likely pay these companies directly. However companies such as Chase or Wells Fargo may have the role of Mortgage Servicer where they deal with the receipt of payments.

The answer is **(D)**

Solution 60

Origination fees are often a percentage of the purchase price, typically 1%. However, this can be worked out and there are instances where it is waived in return for a higher interest rate in which case the fee is paid by means of the yield spread premium.

The answer is **(C)**

Solution 61

The form 1003 requires up to 2 years of employment for each applicant.

The answer is **(B)**

Solution 62

A donor as per Fannie Mae requirements must be a relative by blood, marriage, adoption, or legal guardian. They may not be the builder, the developer, the real estate agent, or any other interested party to the transaction.

The answer is **(D)**

Solution 63

To give the consumer the ability to shop around for the best mortgage, the credit report must group credit checks as a single inquiry for 45 days.

The answer is **(C)**

Solution 64

Due to the early withdrawal penalties and taxes associated with a retirement account, they cannot be considered entirely liquid when evaluating an applicant's reserves.

The answer is **(A)**

Solution 65

Fannie Mae wants to ensure employment is verified as close to closing as possible. In this case, verbal verification can occur no more than 10 days before closing.

The answer is **(A)**

Solution 66

This form is for the borrower to certify that all the information during the application process is accurate to their knowledge. It also allows the lender to sell the loan to another lender and release credit or employment history. It does not indicate anything about the closing disclosure.

The answer is **(C)**

Solution 67

There are 3 types of tolerance thresholds:

- Zero tolerance: As the name implies there may be no increase from estimate to closing disclosure
- 10% cumulative tolerance: The change in all fees must not be more than 10%
- No or unlimited tolerance: Any change is acceptable

The answer is **(A)**

Solution 68

The closing disclosure must be provided 3 business days in advance. Since Sunday is not considered a business day, the answer is Thursday.

The answer is **(C)**

Solution 69

A revised loan estimate must be provided 7 days in advance of consummation.

The answer is **(B)**

Solution 70

The special information pamphlet must be provided within 3 days of the application. If the applicant is denied within the 3 days, the pamphlet needs not to be provided. If the applicant is denied after the 3 days, the pamphlet needs to be provided within the 3-day window.

The answer is **(A)**

Solution 71

HUD provides mortgage counseling and a fee is not applied in all cases. There is not a percentage limit on the fee based on the loan.

The answer is **(C)**

Solution 72

The monthly income must be the yearly income divided by 12. First, find the yearly income:

$$Yearly\ income = 22.52 \times 40 \times 52 = \$46{,}841.60$$

$$Monthly\ income = \frac{46841.60}{12} = \$3903.47$$

The answer is **(A)**

Solution 73

For an application to be received and complete, it must include:

- Consumer name
- Consumer income
- Social Security number
- Property address
- Estimate of the value of the property
- Loan amount sought

The answer is **(A)**

Solution 74

The prepaid section includes insurance, MIP, prepaid interest, and property taxes. In this scenario:

Taxes = (5000)/12 x 3 = 1250
Insurance = 1100/2 = 550
Interest = 17.25 x 10 = 172.50

Sum = $1972

The answer is **(A)**

Solution 75

The "funds for borrower" section is never placed as a positive number. Therefore, despite the calculation being $500, the amount to place is $0. If the calculation is for anything other than a purchase transaction and it comes out negative, then the funds for the borrower are the calculated amount.

The answer is **(A)**

Solution 76

The TIP is the ratio of the total amount of interest paid to the total loan amount:

$$TIP = \left(\frac{100}{200}\right) \times 100 = 50\%$$

The answer is **(B)**

Solution 77

The following are not charges for late payments:

- The right of acceleration
- Fees imposed for actual collection costs
- Referral and extension charges
- Interest charged at the contract rate after the due date

The answer is **(A)**

Solution 78

Any changes that are needed after consummation may be made in a revised closing disclosure within 30 calendar days.

The answer is **(C)**

Solution 79

If a loan does not include an escrow account, estimated property costs must be provided for 1 year.

The answer is **(D)**

Solution 80

Paystubs while necessary for the verification of income, will not provide satisfactory documentation of an earnest money deposit.

The answer is **(C)**

Solution 81

If the gift is determined to be acceptable and is being provided from the donor by wire transfer, documentation of that transfer from the donor is all that is required.

The answer is **(C)**

Solution 82

Sweat equity is work done by the borrower which has value. This work must be listed on the appraisal to be eligible.

The answer is **(A)**

Solution 83

Since the determination of assets and liabilities includes the gross income, federal and state taxes are not considered a liability

The answer is **(C)**

Solution 84

Capital gains must have a 2-year history, and tax returns should be provided for the gains to be considered income.

The answer is **(C)**

Solution 85

The income approach is used to estimate the value of income-producing properties.

The answer is **(B)**

Solution 86

A title search can return a number of issues that may not be readily apparent. Among them are liens, encumbrance, forgeries, boundary disputes, and others. If there is an agreement to access the land, this is called an easement.

The answer is **(C)**

Solution 87

If a property that was previously in a moderate-risk flood area moves to a high-risk area, FEMA now requires flood insurance and will notify the property owner.

The answer is **(A)**

Solution 88

A refinance allows a rescission period of 3 business days.

The answer is **(B)**

Solution 89

Per diem interest is calculated by taking interest on a daily basis. The equation is:

$$Daily\ Interest = \frac{rate}{365} \times pricipal \times time\ period$$

$$Daily\ Interest = \frac{0.0425}{365} \times 242000 \times 30 = \$845.34$$

The answer is **(D)**

Solution 90

Points are a way to pay an up-front amount that will lower the interest rate on a loan. Each point is worth 1% of the loan. In this case, 2 points will cost $6000.

The answer is **(B)**

Solution 91

The new adjustable rate is the index plus the margin: 3 + 2.5 = 5.5%. The new rate is now 0.5% higher than the previous loan. To find the increase, divide the interest rate by the number of months and multiply by the balance:

$$Monthly\ Interest\ Increase = \frac{0.005}{12} \times 158000 = \$65.83$$

The answer is **(A)**

Solution 92

The combined LTV is simply a ratio of the addition of the loans to the addition of the values. In this case, we want the overall LTV to be at least 80% so the equation becomes:

$$0.80 = \frac{Loan\ 1 + Loan\ 2}{Value\ 1 + Value\ 2} = \frac{230000 + Loan\ 2}{280000 + 220000}; Loan\ 2 = \$170,000$$

The down payment is then $220,000 - $170,000 = $50,000

The percent is 50000/220000 = 22.7%

The answer is **(D)**

Solution 93

FHA maximum debt ratios are 31 on the front end and 43 on the back end.

The answer is **(B)**

Solution 94

The margin for an ARM most likely will remain the same over time but the index is subject to change.

The answer is **(B)**

Solution 95

Any large deposit which is not consistent with a borrower's income patterns must be documented if it is greater than 2% of the sale price.

The answer is **(B)**

Solution 96

USDA loans are more lenient in employment history than others. There is no minimum length of time requirement in a current position.

The answer is **(A)**

Solution 97

There are three rules as established by the Gramm-Leach Bliley Act:

- The Financial Privacy Rule: requires providing customers with privacy disclosure

- Safeguard Rule: Requires written security plans by institutions
- Pretexting Prohibition: Prohibits the practice of collecting information under false pretenses

The answer is **(A)**

Solution 98

Section 10 of RESPA stipulates that the lender may require a cushion for an escrow account no more than 1/6 of the total yearly disbursements.

The answer is **(B)**

Solution 99

The sales contract does not go into detail on the credit history of the applicant. While a recently issued Social Security number may be an issue, it is not related to the sales contract.

The answer is **(D)**

Solution 100

For a product which is bona fide, it must be able to be purchased by the consumer and not disparaged in any way by the advertiser. The seller may show other products that are available, but the original offer must also be available.

The answer is **(B)**

Solution 101

The specific exemptions to the Fair Housing Act are:

- Rental of a room in a dwelling with no more than four independent units
- Housing operated by private organizations or clubs which restrict membership
- Single-family purchase without a mortgage broker

The answer is **(D)**

Solution 102

As per the Consumer Protection Financial Bureau, the majority of complaints are related to mortgage services, about 80%.

The answer is **(A)**

Solution 103

The loan officer has specific duties in preparing the application from the borrower to the lender. They do not have a role in approval.

The answer is **(B)**

Solution 104

Flipping is when a borrower is encouraged to refinance without any real benefit. This results in unnecessary additional fees and costs.

The answer is **(C)**

Solution 105

The attorney fee cannot be charged by the lender and is not allowable.

The answer is **(B)**

Solution 106

When a power of attorney is used, a person named the principal grants the authority to someone else to act on their behalf.

The answer is **(A)**

Solution 107

There is no duration requirement for the marriage, but the lender can run a credit report if the spouse is permitted on the account, contractually liable for the account, or the spouse's income is used on the basis of payment.

The answer is **(D)**

Solution 108

SAFE requires there to be a process in place for the licensing of MLO's which includes

- criminal history and credit background checks
- pre-licensure education
- pre-licensure testing
- continuing education
- net worth, surety bond, or recovery fund

The answer is **(C)**

Solution 109

The Loan Origination Rule dictates regulations related to compensation. These include:

- Barring compensation from being determined by the terms of the transaction or a proxy for a transaction term.
- Bonuses, retirement plans, and other compensation plans that are based on mortgage-related profits are permitted.
- Barring compensation by the consumer and another person. As an example, a creditor.

The answer is **(B)**

Solution 110

CFPB civil penalties are assessed no more than the prescribed maximum per day that the violation continues.

The answer is **(D)**

Solution 111

The characteristics of NMLS identifiers can be found on the website. Once assigned the number cannot be changed.

The answer is **(A)**

Solution 112

The SAFE Act requires MLO's of Federally regulated institutions to submit to the Registry:

- Identifying information. This includes
    - Name,
    - Home address
    - Social security number
    - Gender
    - Date of birth
    - Principal business address
- Employment history for 10 years previous
- Disclosure of any regulatory actions
- Fingerprints for an FBI background check.

The answer is **(D)**

Solution 113

The NMLS Registry has a number of functions and the minimum requirements are outlined in section 1008.301 of Regulation H. The goals include uniform licensed applications and do not encourage individualized

The answer is **(C)**

Solution 114

All agencies have adopted the language which indicates that identifiers shall be provided to consumers 1) Upon request 2) Before acting as a mortgage loan officer 3) Through any initial written communication.

The answer is **(D)**

Solution 115

The licensed mortgage originator has more requirements than a registered one including the pre-license requirement.

The answer is **(D)**

Solution 116

Flipping which is commonly confused with house flipping by a contractor, is when collusion occurs between a buyer, appraiser, and potential a lender in which a home is bought and then sold artificially for a higher price in a short time frame.

The answer is **(B)**

Solution 117

The definition of a "loan originator" can be defined by the actions taken by the person and cover a broad spectrum of activity as defined Loan Origination Rule. One of the tasks that can fall outside of the definition is clerical or administrative work related to the application.

The answer is **(A)**

Solution 118

In order for settlement services to be offered at a discount in a combination, the following must apply:

- The use of the combination must be optional and
- The discount cannot be made up for elsewhere

The answer is **(A)**

Solution 119

Material misrepresentation is the intentional hiding or altering of a material fact such as income or tax statements. Material misstatements are untrue statements related to intention or financial status. Omission is the intentional leaving out of information.

The answer is **(A)**

Solution 120

Since the rate can adjust, the applicant must be evaluated on the anticipation of a changing rate. Therefore, the ability to repay is based on the greater of the initial rate and the fully indexed rate.

The answer is **(C)**

Solution 121

Safe Harbor protects the loan originator in the event that a consumer takes legal action. Safe Harbor says that if the loan can be determined to be a qualified loan then the mortgage complies with ATR requirements. Higher-priced loans however are exempt from safe harbor.

The answer is **(A)**

Solution 122

The CFPB has a number of functions related to consumer protection. They do not dictate the actions of consumers.

The answer is **(D)**

Solution 123

A consumer has 60 days to provide feedback to the company's response.

The answer is **(D)**

Solution 124

The minimum length of an escrow account for higher-priced mortgages was lengthened to 5 years as per the TILA Escrow Rule.

The answer is **(C)**

Solution 125

Section 1022.25 covers reasonable methods of opting-out. They do not include requiring the consumer to produce a letter of their own.

The answer is **(A)**

Solution 126

Required use refers to a situation in which there is a requirement to use a person referred by one settlement service for another. A person must have the right to choose freely who will provide their services.

The answer is **(B)**

Solution 127

RESPA section 1024.7(a)(4) indicates that a fee for the mortgage broker is only permittable as a condition for providing an estimate related to the cost of a credit report. This is at the option of the broker.

The answer is **(C)**

Solution 128

As per section 1024.7(f)(4), the GFE expires after a time period of 10 days or a number specified previously if the borrower does not express an intent to continue.

The answer is **(B)**

Solution 129

RESPA 1024.7(e) provides permittable charges which must not exceed those on the estimate as well as those which can be within 10%.

The answer is **(C)**

Solution 130

Section 1002.2(o) defines the age of an elderly person as 62.

The answer is **(A)**

Solution 131

As per section 1002.9(a), notice shall be provided within 30 days after adverse action is taken on an existing account.

The answer is **(B)**

Solution 132

Section 1002.6(b)(5) provides guidance on what income to be considered as a part of the applicant's creditworthiness. The creditor must include all sources of income including part-time wages, pensions, alimony, etc. but does have the ability to evaluate the inclusion of income on the basis of its likelihood to continue.

The answer is **(C)**

Solution 133

The requirements for the cosigner must follow all of the restrictions of discrimination in regard to sex, marital status, race, and others. The creditor can however dictate certain stipulations such as the location of the cosigner in relation to the applicant. This is outlined in section 1002.7(d)(5).

The answer is **(A)**

Solution 134

TILA Section 1026.15(b) indicates that a creditor shall distribute two hard copies to each consumer.

The answer is **(B)**

Solution 135

TILA section 1026.24(i) provides prohibited acts in advertising. In this situation, we are directed specifically to section 1026.24(i)(1)(ii) which discusses non-variable-rate transactions and the term fixed. The requirement is that any use of the term "fixed" shall be accompanied by the time period for which the rate or payment is fixed and the fact that the rate may vary.

The answer is **(D)**

Solution 136

A balloon loan must have a minimum of 5 years unless it is considered a bridge loan.

The answer is **(B)**

Solution 137

If the APR for your transaction is more than 6.5 or 8.5 percentage points higher than the APOR, then the transaction qualifies as a high-cost mortgage. In this case, since it is a first lien, the APR will be the APOR plus 6.5% which will be 12%.

The answer is **(D)**

Solution 138

Higher-priced mortgages are required to establish an escrow account except for the exceptions outlined in section 1026.35(b)(2). A bridge loan with a term of less than 12 months is acceptable, but a loan of less than 5 years is not.

The answer is **(B)**

Solution 139

TILA section 1026.36(e) covers the prohibition of steering a consumer towards a specific loan type or transaction. The consumer must be presented with the loan options in section 3 which include:

"A. The loan with the lowest interest rate;

B. The loan with the lowest interest rate without negative amortization, a prepayment penalty, interest-only payments, a balloon payment in the first 7 years of the life of the loan, a demand feature, shared equity, or shared appreciation; or, in the case of a reverse mortgage, a loan without a prepayment penalty, or shared equity or shared appreciation; and

C. The loan with the lowest total dollar amount of discount points, origination points, or origination fees (or, if two or more loans have the same total dollar amount of discount points, origination points, or origination fees, the loan with the lowest interest rate that has the lowest total dollar amount of discount points, origination points or origination fees)."

While origination fees are a part of option "C" a loan with solely the lowest origination fees is not required.

The answer is **(D)**

Solution 140

As per HMDA section 1003.2(f), a mixed-use property can be considered under the definition of a dwelling if it is determined that its primary purpose is residential. In this case, using a percentage calculation, the primary purpose is commercial and therefore does not comply.

The answer is **(A)**

Solution 141

For a chapter 13 bankruptcy, the length of time is 7 years. For chapter 7, it is 10 years.

The answer is **(B)**

Solution 142

Not all creditors are subject to the "red flag" rule. A business has to evaluate if the following scenarios apply:

- Is there a deferred payment for goods and services or bill customers?
- Do they grant or arrange credit?
- Do they participate in the decision to extend, renew, or set the terms of credit?

A business that does not defer payment does not fit the qualifications.

The answer is **(A)**

Solution 143

Information is publicly available if an institution has a reasonable basis to believe that the information is lawfully available to the general public. A phone book fits this description.

The answer is **(A)**

Solution 144

The consumer must have the option to use and receive paper copies as well as information regarding the right to withdraw and any consequences associated. The process of E-signing is not a requirement.

The answer is **(B)**

Solution 145

Section 325 of the US Patriot Act covers concentration account requirements at financial institutions. There is no restriction on the number of transactions.

The answer is **(D)**

Solution 146

The Good Neighbor Next Door program allows these types of professionals to seek discounted properties in specific areas.

The answer is **(C)**

Solution 147

The Fair Housing Act protects the rights of any individual against discrimination related to housing.

The answer is **(D)**

Solution 148

The Homeownership counseling act is not eligible for those that are assisted by the Farmer Home Administration.

The answer is **(B)**

Solution 149

Loans that are exempt from ATR/QM are:

- Open-end credit plans

- Time-share plans
- Reverse mortgage
- Bridge loans
- Short duration construction-to-permanent loans
- Consumer credit transactions secured by vacant land

The answer is **(D)**

Solution 150

Type 2 QM loans are temporary and must meet one of the requirements listed except for insurance by the USDA.

The answer is **(D)**

Solution 151

For any FHA loan, the seller concessions are capped at 6%.

The answer is **(C)**

Solution 152

Loan Level Price Adjustments (LLPA's) are fees assessed according to an evaluation of how risky a loan is according to Fannie Mae and Freddie Mac. These fees, however, do not apply to FHA, USDA, or VA loans

The answer is **(A)**

Solution 153

There are a number of different options for automated underwriting systems. Fannie Mae uses Desktop Underwriter while Freddie Mac uses Loan Prospector.

The answer is **(A)**

Solution 154

The VA loan allows the borrower to put down no money.

The answer is **(B)**

Solution 155

The hazard insurance must show that it fully covers damage from natural occurrences. This may include an endorsement or separate policy from the original. The claims must be settled however on a replacement cost basis and not actual value.

The answer is **(B)**

Solution 156

A prepayment penalty is capped at 2% for the first two years and 1% thereafter.

The answer is **(B)**

Solution 157

The amount of the VA fee depends on the type of service and the amount of the down payment. For the scenario listed, it will be 1.75%

The answer is **(C)**

Solution 158

The residual income is simply the amount leftover after monthly expenses. In this case 6000 – 1200 – 400 – 200 = $4200.

The answer is **(A)**

Solution 159

While a down payment of 20% can avoid the need for PMI and a borrower can apply to have PMI removed at 80% LTV, it will automatically stop at 78%.

The answer is **(B)**

Solution 160

One of the main concerns that makes a jumbo loan risky is that since it falls outside of the requirements of Fannie Mae and Freddie Mac, it is not backed by the government and the lender is not protected from losses.

The answer is **(A)**

Solution 161

Payment shock is the concern for the difference in a person's current financial obligations and the proposed ones. It is often a concern when someone has no previous mortgage experience such as a first-time buyer or current renter, or when the loan may fluctuate over its life in cases such as adjustable rates.

The answer is **(D)**

Solution 162

Debt to income (DTI) ratio is a comparison of a borrower's income to obligations. In this case, we know the target ratio and we have to back figure the maximum mortgage:

$$DTI = \frac{(Mortgage + Debt\ Payments)}{Monthly\ Income} = 0.40 = \frac{(Mortgage + 800)}{5750}; Mortgage = \$1500$$

The answer is **(B)**

Solution 163

The adjustable-rate is the margin plus the index once the fixed period has ended. In this scenario it is 2 + 4 = 6%

The answer is **(C)**

Solution 164

There are a number of indexes used in the determination of rates however the Consumer Price Index is related more so to the sale of consumer goods

The answer is **(D)**

Solution 165

There are situations where income does not need to be verified to be approved for a loan. No-income loans are for specific for such situations. In the example presented, the borrower is not receiving paychecks and all of his assets are in a business account and not a personal account. In this case, both the assets and the income are not verifiable, but the lender has reasonable cause to believe the borrower can pay back the loan. The borrower is only stating both income and assets.

The answer is **(A)**

Solution 166

Non-qualified loans are those which do not fit the requirements of qualified loans. They are not necessarily high-risk loans however and there are certain circumstances where they are appropriate. They may be for self-employed borrowers but typically with a short history, often less than 2 years. While the requirements are different from qualified mortgages, a minimum credit score is still required. Non-QM's can also be for loans greater than 30 years or a high DTI but a demonstration that they can be made up for with substantial reserves.

The answer is **(B)**

Solution 167

A purchase money second mortgage is used typically in lieu of a down payment for a home purchase. It is a second, separate loan that can enable a borrower to finance up to 100% of the home.

The answer is **(A)**

Solution 168

For a fixed-rate mortgage, there is no fluctuation in the mortgage payment due to interest or principal payments for the life of the loan. The total may fluctuate based on property taxes, hazard insurance, or PMI.

The answer is **(C)**

Solution 169

ARM's have caps that the rate cannot exceed regardless of the index and margin. The lifetime cap limits the increase over the life of the loan and the periodic cap limits the increase from one period to the next. In this case for year seven the margin plus index is 4 + 2 = 6%. Then in year eight the margin plus index is 6 + 2 = 8%. This is under the lifetime cap of 5 + 4 = 9% but the increase from 6 to 8 is more than the periodic cap so it is limited to 7.5%.

The answer is **(C)**

Solution 170

A creditor must notify the borrower at least 210 days in advance but no more than 240 days for the first-rate change.

The answer is **(A)**

Solution 171

HELOC's vs. home equity loans are similar in that the borrower accesses funds from the equity in the existing home, but there are some differences. One of which is that the home equity loan typically will have a fixed rate while the HELOC will be an adjustable rate.

The answer is **(C)**

Solution 172

The qualification for a reverse mortgage depends on a number of factors including age and interest rates. However, an applicant does not need 100% equity to be considered for a reverse mortgage. The requirement is you must be able to pay off your existing mortgage with the amount received. Therefore, if you owe half, you can pay it off with the other half.

The answer is **(A)**

Solution 173

A construction only loan is actually two separate loans: one solely for the construction of the home and then a mortgage. Because of this the fees for the loans are separate and require two sets

The answer is **(D)**

Solution 174

If a bank provides a notice of default but the borrower still has time to rectify the situation, the home is in the pre-foreclosure state.

The answer is **(C)**

Solution 175

The spread premium must be disclosed as a part of the HUD-1 form.

The answer is **(A)**

Solution 176

The first-year rate can be no more than 2% less than the original rate.

The answer is **(D)**

Solution 177

A cash-out refinance is the same as a normal refinance except the borrower taps into the existing equity and receives a lump sum of a specified amount above the existing principal balance.

The answer is **(B)**

Solution 178

A fee simple provides no further stipulations on the transfer.

The answer is **(B)**

Solution 179

A third-party provider is an authorized online service provider. The PISP allows online payments without the need for card details. The AISP allows the viewing of specific account information.

The answer is **(B)**

Solution 180

The secondary mortgage market is where mortgages are bought and sold as securities. An aggregator is an entity that purchases mortgages from financial institutions and then securitizes them into mortgage-backed securities (MBS).

The answer is **(D)**

Solution 181

An assumable loan allows a borrower to take on an existing loan including all aspects of that loan including the interest rate.

The answer is **(A)**

Solution 182

If a borrower is to use a gift to cover costs on a mortgage, there are situations in which there must be a contribution from the borrower's own funds. For an LTV of 80% or greater and a two- or four-unit home, the borrower must contribute 5%. Otherwise, the requirement is 0%

The answer is **(A)**

Solution 183

Liquid assets are typically considered seasoned if they remain in an account for 60 days or more.

The answer is **(A)**

Solution 184

Since a lender cannot verify the employment status of a self-employed individual through a company, they need to see the history of income and determine if it is viable and likely to continue. This can be done most often by reviewing the tax return.

The answer is **(D)**

Solution 185

For the 10% cumulative rule all of the fees combined must not increase by more than 10%: 5000 x 1.1 = $5500.

The answer is **(B)**

Solution 186

A decrease in a fee does not count in the cumulation of recording fees. Only increases are counted.

The answer is **(A)**

Solution 187

TRID stipulates that the lender must deliver the application no later than 3 business days after application.

The answer is **(A)**

Solution 188

The Loan estimate provides a number of details for the loan including rates, taxes, and fees. The inspection is separate and while very common and recommended, it is not a requirement always.

The answer is **(C)**

Solution 189

The loan estimate expires 10 days after issuing.

The answer is **(A)**

Solution 190

An increase in assets does not negatively impact the consumer's eligibility for the loan and therefore is not a valid reason.

The answer is **(A)**

Solution 191

There are three changes that will initiate a new 3-day waiting period. They are:

- A change to the interest rate
- The APR changes by more than 1/8 of a percent or ¼ of a percent depending on the rate type
- A prepayment penalty is added

The answer is **(B)**

Solution 192

The exceptions for providing the special information pamphlet are in section 1024.6(a)(3) and are:

- Refinance
- Closed-end loans
- Reverse mortgages
- Any other federally related mortgage loan whose purpose is not the purchase of a 1-4 family residential property

The answer is **(C)**

Solution 193

The 10% cumulative tolerance applies to both recording fees and third-party services. The third-party charge however is not included if the consumer chooses someone outside of the written provided list.

The answer is **(D)**

Solution 194

HUD approved counselor's help with services related to the ability to pay a mortgage for a borrower. There is no HUD hotline, however.

The answer is **(C)**

Solution 195

Amounts shall be rounded to the nearest whole dollar

The answer is **(C)**

Solution 196

The "Other" section of the closing disclosure is the area for costs that are not required to be disclosed on the loan estimate. These include brokerage fees, inspection fees, home warranties, and others.

The answer is **(B)**

Solution 197

The notice for the right to rescind is not required when the loan is for a purchase. This is provided for other types of loans such as a refinance or HELOC

The answer is **(C)**

Solution 198

The holidays which are not considered business days are as detailed in 5 U.S.C 6103(a). The Friday after Thanksgiving, while many have off is not a federal holiday

The answer is **(B)**

Solution 199

The estimated cash to close is the sum of the cost minus any previous deposits or seller credits. In this case: 8200 + 19500 – 5000 = $22700.

The answer is **(C)**

Solution 200

Verification is needed if it exceeds 2% of the sale price.

The answer is **(B)**

Solution 201

Social security must be considered likely to continue beyond 3 years.

The answer is **(A)**

Solution 202

For an FHA loan, if there are gaps in the employment history then there is a 6-month minimum for verification of employment at the current job.

The answer is **(B)**

Solution 203

Income has no effect on credit score.

The answer is **(A)**

Solution 204

The housing ratio also known as the front-end ratio is the housing payment divided by the monthly income. The monthly income is 60000/12 = 5000. The equation becomes:

$$0.28 = \left(\frac{450 + 90 + 120 + Mortgage\ Payment}{5000}\right)$$

If you solve for the mortgage payment you get $740.

The answer is **(A)**

Solution 205

For a building that is not frequently sold, the cost approach determines what the value of the property may be by assuming a reasonable buyer would not pay more than a comparable building on a comparable lot. Often this is most appropriate for buildings such as schools, hospitals, or government buildings which are not bought and sold frequently.

The answer is **(C)**

Solution 206

The right to receive notice must be provided within 3 business days.

The answer is **(A)**

Solution 207

Just because a document or source discusses a property's value does not mean it can be used as a valuation. This is certainly true for public information.

The answer is **(D)**

Solution 208

An appraiser must not be influenced in any way to make a decision. They may, however, be alerted to additional information.

The answer is **(C)**

Solution 209

Choosing comparable properties does not have exact requirements but should be as close as possible in size, location, age, and other characteristics. The comparable homes should also be sold as recently as possible. Of the options listed, an age difference of 35 years is a noticeable gap and should not be used as a comparable based on the information provided.

The answer is **(C)**

Solution 210

The title report may be obtained through any means desired by the purchaser. It can be done personally at the assessor's office or courthouse but most often it is obtained through a professional.

The answer is **(D)**

Solution 211

FEMA requirements stipulate that the flood coverage must be at least the lesser of:

- The maximum amount of NFIP coverage available for the particular property type, or
- The outstanding principal balance of the loan, or
- The insurable value of the structure.

The answer is **(B)**

Solution 212

If there is no insurance on a property due to reasons such as failure to pay, the lender can force insurance on the borrower so that the property is still protected. This is known as force-placed insurance.

The answer is **(C)**

Solution 213

PMI is used as protection for the lender. The borrower is in no way protected if there is a failure to pay the monthly payments.

The answer is **(A)**

Solution 214

Despite the fact that a loan may have the necessary equity to remove PMI, if it is not absent at the origination of the loan, there is a seasoning period in which the borrower must wait to apply to remove the payment. This period is a minimum of 2 years.

The answer is **(B)**

Solution 215

For a purchase, there is no right to rescind after closing.

The answer is **(A)**

Solution 216

All of the options listed must be satisfied except for a notice of payoff.

The answer is **(B)**

Solution 217

Points are used to lower interest rates and each point will lower the rate by 0.25%.

The answer is **(A)**

Solution 218

Monthly payment = 820 + 1200/12 + 6000/12 + 82 = $1502.

The answer is **(B)**

Solution 219

PMI can be removed if the LTV is 80%. In this case the closing costs of the refinance are rolled into the loan and must be added to the existing principal = 340,000 + 4000 = $344,000. To get the LTV, divide by 0.80: 344,000/0.8 = $430,000.

The answer is **(B)**

Solution 220

Fannie Mae allows the DTI to be a maximum of 36% for manually underwritten loans. Anything above that must be evaluated further up to a maximum of 45%.

The answer is **(A)**

Solution 221

The GLBA provides guidance to institutions regarding the sharing of non-public information. They must at a minimum disclose:

- What information is collected about its customers
- With whom the financial institution shares the information
- How the information is protected
- Opt-out options

The answer is **(A)**

Solution 222

Redlining is the unethical practice of not providing services to residents of a certain area based on race or ethnicity. The Community Reinvestment Act in 1977 was passed to prevent these practices.

The answer is **(C)**

Solution 223

The loan processor provides final approval of a loan application before going to the lender. They will check for red flags and ensure all information is verifiable.

The answer is **(C)**

Solution 224

Fannie Mae provides a list of potential red flags with some labeled as high-level. These are red-flags which more than likely need significant investigation. Address discrepancies are not acceptable on a loan considering it is for the sale of a property.

The answer is **(A)**

Solution 225

Occupancy fraud is related to the applicant lying about the home being owner-occupied. An owner-occupied home can often get lower interest rates than investment properties.

The answer is **(B)**

Solution 226

When an attractive product is presented to get a potential customer engaged but then is sold a different product, this is a bait and switch.

The answer is **(C)**

Solution 227

The Fair Housing Act requires advertisements to make the consumer aware of the seller's participation in the requirements of equal housing lending. They do not need to go into detail of what the Act requires in ads.

The answer is **(A)**

Solution 228

When a professional takes advantage of an ill-informed borrower for personal gain, this is called predatory lending.

The answer is **(A)**

Solution 229

Steering is forcing a specific geographical area on an applicant based on race, religion, or ethnicity and it is strictly prohibited.

The answer is **(A)**

Solution 230

The Home Mortgage Disclosure Act applies to residential loans including:

- Purchase
- Refinance
- Home improvement
- Subordinate financing

It does not apply to the purchase of vacant land or a construction loan

The answer is **(B)**

Solution 231

There are three tiers increasing in severity from one to three. The third includes those who knowingly commit violations.

The answer is **(C)**

Solution 232

As per section 1008.107 of Regulation H, the minimum annual license renewal requires 8 hours of continuing education.

The answer is **(B)**

Solution 233

As per section 1008.105, a felony that does not include fraud, dishonesty, a breach of trust, or money laundering includes a waiting period of 7 years.

The answer is **(C)**

Solution 234

Section 1008.103(b) describes the actions which constitute the business of a loan originator. Pre-approval services are not included.

The answer is **(D)**

Solution 235

The records shall be provided for review at any time.

The answer is **(A)**

Solution 236

The public comment period must last no more than 30 days.

The answer is **(C)**

Solution 237

The license expires after 5 years.

The answer is **(B)**

Solution 238

Violating section 8 can bring up to one year in prison or up to a $10,000 fine.

The answer is **(A)**

Solution 239

Fraud which is intentional is actual fraud.

The answer is **(A)**

Solution 240

It is acceptable for a consumer to obtain multiple appraisals

The answer is **(C)**

Solution 241

FHA requires 3 months before the resale of a home.

The answer is **(A)**

Solution 242

The ECOA requires the lender or mortgage broker to consider reliable sources of income such as part-time, pensions, alimony, social security, public assistance, and others. However, the applicant is not required to submit alimony, child support, or separate maintenance as income.

The answer is **(A)**

Solution 243

As per section 1026.43(c)(2)-4, there are eight factors that must be considered for a good faith ATR evaluation:

- Current or reasonably expected income
- Employment status
- Monthly mortgage payment
- Simultaneous loans
- Monthly property taxes and insurance
- Debts, alimony, and child support
- DTI ratios
- Credit history

Other factors may be considered but these are the minimum requirements

The answer is **(D)**

Solution 244

Rebuttable presumption is legal protection against consumers taking action on higher-priced mortgages. If the court determines the loan was a higher-priced QM the consumer still has a chance to argue but the lender is protected. This is an additional protection beyond ATR requirements but less than Safe Harbor.

The answer is **(D)**

Solution 245

Public information for complaints includes the date, subject, and a description if consented. There is no mention of penalties, but the resolution of the complaint is indicated

The answer is **(D)**

Solution 246

A continuing relationship must include transactions that occur over a period of time. Isolated transactions would not fulfill the requirements such as travel insurance which is purchased only once.

The answer is **(D)**

Solution 247

Part 681 covers the requirements for identity theft rules regarding identity theft. The institution must identify and respond to red flags but is not required to cover the consumer.

The answer is **(B)**

Solution 248

The VA cash-out loan allows the borrower to take out 100% equity.

The answer is **(D)**

Solution 249

Discount points can be applied but are only applicable to the fixed rate. They are often less expensive than fixed-rate mortgage points given the shorter time period. Some lenders will allow points on the margin which would affect the variable rate.

The answer is **(A)**

Solution 250

The APR includes the interest rate and any additional costs rolled into the loan such as discount points, underwriting fees, settlement fees, etc. The appraisal is most often paid directly by the buyer and not included.

The answer is **(C)**

PDF Version Access

1. Go to https://www.bovabooks.com/nmls-pdf

2. Click Download

3. Email us at info@bovabooks.com with any questions

4. Leave us a review on Amazon

Answer Key

1	C	41	C	81	C	121	A	161	D	201	A	241	A
2	A	42	C	82	A	122	D	162	B	202	B	242	A
3	C	43	C	83	C	123	D	163	C	203	A	243	D
4	C	44	B	84	C	124	C	164	D	204	A	244	D
5	A	45	B	85	B	125	A	165	A	205	C	245	D
6	D	46	C	86	C	126	B	166	B	206	A	246	D
7	B	47	A	87	A	127	C	167	A	207	D	247	B
8	B	48	D	88	B	128	B	168	C	208	C	248	D
9	C	49	C	89	D	129	C	169	C	209	C	249	A
10	A	50	D	90	B	130	A	170	A	210	D	250	C
11	B	51	C	91	A	131	B	171	C	211	B		
12	B	52	D	92	D	132	C	172	A	212	C		
13	D	53	A	93	B	133	A	173	D	213	A		
14	D	54	C	94	B	134	B	174	C	214	B		
15	B	55	C	95	B	135	D	175	A	215	A		
16	D	56	A	96	A	136	B	176	D	216	B		
17	B	57	B	97	A	137	D	177	B	217	A		
18	C	58	A	98	B	138	B	178	B	218	B		
19	C	59	D	99	D	139	D	179	B	219	B		
20	B	60	C	100	B	140	A	180	D	220	A		
21	C	61	B	101	D	141	B	181	A	221	A		
22	C	62	D	102	A	142	A	182	A	222	C		
23	D	63	C	103	B	143	A	183	A	223	C		
24	C	64	A	104	C	144	B	184	D	224	A		
25	A	65	A	105	B	145	D	185	B	225	B		
26	A	66	C	106	A	146	C	186	A	226	C		
27	B	67	A	107	D	147	D	187	A	227	A		
28	A	68	C	108	C	148	B	188	C	228	A		
29	B	69	B	109	B	149	D	189	A	229	A		
30	D	70	A	110	D	150	D	190	A	230	B		
31	A	71	C	111	A	151	C	191	B	231	C		
32	C	72	A	112	D	152	A	192	C	232	B		
33	C	73	A	113	C	153	A	193	D	233	C		
34	C	74	A	114	D	154	B	194	C	234	D		
35	A	75	A	115	D	155	B	195	C	235	A		
36	D	76	B	116	B	156	B	196	B	236	C		
37	C	77	A	117	A	157	C	197	C	237	B		
38	B	78	C	118	A	158	A	198	B	238	A		
39	C	79	D	119	A	159	B	199	C	239	A		
40	A	80	C	120	C	160	A	200	B	240	C		

Thank You Again for Your Purchase!

What Did You Think of the Study Guide?

It is a long and difficult road to passing and we are extremely grateful you chose us to help along the way. We hope that it added value and efficiency to your studying. We are here for any questions or concerns you may have and we will respond quickly if you email us at:

Bovabooks@gmail.com

If you enjoyed this book, it would help greatly if you have the time to **leave a positive review on our Amazon product page**. Reviews help to support small businesses like ours.

Made in the USA
Las Vegas, NV
23 June 2024